MIDNIGHT'S ALL A GLIMMER

Poetry, Personality, and the Power to See

AN ANTHOLOGY

KAREN VAN ZINO

Midnight's All A Glimmer

Published by:

Sassafras Press
822 Hartz Way
Suite 205
Danville, CA 94526

info@KarenVanZinoMD.com

First Printing, 2018

Printed in the United States of America

ISBN: 978-0-9842374-4-9

Cover Design by Leslie Sears
Drawings by Gina Rico

Epigraph

What is light in me illume,
What is low raise and support
~ John Milton
Paradise Lost Book I

True Poetry is
Like the Loadstone
Which both Attracts
The Needle and
Supplies it With
Magnetic Power
~ from the Bronze Doors
of the Boston Public Library

'Tis Thine
The Prime and Vital Principle is there
In the recesses of thy nature.
~ William Wordsworth

Contents

Dedication

In Loving Memory
of
David Daniels, M.D.
(1934-2017)

Healer, Pioneer, Teacher,
Mentor & Friend

Acknowledgements

I am deeply indebted to the scholarly work of Don Richard Riso and Russ Hudson and their teachings at the Enneagram Institute. Their seminal books on the Enneagram: *Personality Types, Understanding the Enneagram,* and *The Wisdom of the Enneagram* are foundational to the Enneagram descriptions in this volume. I am equally indebted to Roxanne Howe-Murphy EdD for her brilliant synthesis of the Riso-Hudson teachings and her original work in her volumes: *Deep Coaching: Using the Enneagram for Profound Change* and *Deep Living.* My choice to organize the nine types around the Social Styles is a direct tribute to Roxanne's clarity of teaching. Her guidance as a founding teacher of the Deep Coaching Institute and her personal mentorship of my spiritual journey have changed my life. A warm thanks to Enneagram teacher and Coach Michael Naylor for teaching me that writing is a spiritual exercise. I have also benefited greatly working with Enneagram teachers Gayle Scott, Lynda Roberts, Andrea Isaacs, Belinda Gore and Diana Redmond, and the fine teachers with the Narrative Tradition School, most especially the late David Daniels, MD.

My thanks to Susan Hansch, friend beyond measure, cannot be expressed in sufficient superlatives in appreciation for her support from the initial germ of my idea to her painstaking reading of every word of the manuscript. In the days of self-doubt and screaming inner critic voices she was there, listening and encouraging.

To my women warrior friends Nadine Oei, Linda Bosserman, and Gloria Soto-Reyes and to all of my Deep Coaching colleagues and believers and to my amazing daughters Monica Rico, Ramona Rico, Gina

Rico, and Joanna Rico I say a hearty thank you. They have all stood by me helping me to laugh along the way. Special thanks to Gina for providing the book's wonderful drawings.

To Mike Rounds of Rounds, Miller and Associates who formatted this volume and saw it to press — Mike, you are the best cheerleader and one of the most generous men I've ever met.

My everlasting gratitude goes to my dad Anthony J. Van Zino, poet and gardener of Jersey tomatoes par excellence. You fed me in more ways than one. To my beloved husband Frank Rico, the quiet man who offered the foundation and space allowing me to bring my dream into reality — I am forever grateful.

Preface

Why I Wrote this Book

I love the power of poetry and I love the wisdom of the Enneagram. Both help me to understand my place in this life and both are vital to my health. This volume is the result of bringing these two passions together. Each enriches the other and together they offer the reader a way to understand his or her greatest gifts as well as greatest challenges.

The seed for this book began to sprout one clear spring day several years ago as I was driving to the Monterey Peninsula for my first ever solo overnight retreat. It took lots of encouragement from my mentor, coach and teacher Roxanne to get me to this point; for taking time away from all the people in my life to be alone, time with just myself, seemed not only foreign but downright selfish. Who was I really if I wasn't tending to all the people in my busy life — family, patients, students, and friends. I had been working with Roxanne over the previous months exploring the muddle I was in. I felt stuck, like something was missing but I didn't know what. I had steadfastly resisted her suggestions to take a day and night away and be with myself. On the surface it had seemed absurd even to me that I was so resistant, yet I was loathe to leave everyone who depended upon me, even for a day and a night. It was a poem that broke through my resistance and set me on my way.

I'd been given a recording of poems written and read by modern poet David Whyte whom I'd never heard of before. The poems were from his West of Ireland series and Whyte, who was born and raised on the moors of northern England, his mother an

Irishwoman and his father a Yorkshireman, talked about the poems and read them in his mellifluous Yorkshire/Irish tongue. Driving down the 680 freeway with green hills to either side of me I listened, mesmerized as Whyte read the poem "Coleman's Bed." He had explained who Coleman was—an early Celtic saint who wandered the hills of Western Ireland teaching. He would sleep each night nestled into a shallow hollow of rocks high up in the hills. The site was now known as 'Coleman's Bed' and Whyte had visited it often. He spoke of another Celtic saint, St. Kevin who, like St. Francis of Assisi, was a tender lover of animals and a calm and steady presence for others. A legend told of how, while praying with outstretched arms, a blackbird laid her eggs in Kevin's palm and he remained there, arms open, for days until the baby birds were hatched. This image touched me deeply.

During my two hour drive to Monterey I listened over and over again to this poem and when I parked along the shoreline of the Pacific Ocean's Asilomar Beach I sat in my car and transcribed the words into a little red notebook I carried with me. I can hear and feel the cadence of words in his rich tones still. Here is the poem that awakened me to my deeper self and shone a light on what was being called forth.

COLEMAN'S BED

Make a nesting now, a place to which
the birds can come, think of Kevin's
prayerful palm holding the blackbird's egg
and be the one, looking out from this place
who warms interior forms into light.
Feel the way the cliff at your back
gives shelter to your outward view,
then bring from those horizons

all discordant elements that seek a home.

Be taught now, among the trees and rocks,
how the discarded is woven into shelter,
learn the way things hidden and unspoken
slowly proclaim their voice in the world.
Find that far inward symmetry
to all outward appearances, apprentice
yourself to yourself, begin to welcome back
all you sent away, be a new annunciation,
make yourself a door through which
to be hospitable, even to the stranger in you.

See with every turning day,
how each season makes a child
of you again, wants you to become
a seeker after rainfall and birdsong,
watch how it weathers you to a testing
in the tried and true, tells you
with each falling leaf, to leave and slip away,
even from the branch that held you,
to go when you need to, to be courageous,
to be like a last word you'd want to say
before you leave the world.

Above all, be alone with it all,
a hiving off, a corner of silence
amidst the noise, refuse to talk,
even to yourself, and stay in this place
until the current of the story
is strong enough to float you out.

Goest then, to where others
in this place have come before,
under the hazel, by the ruined chapel,

below the cave where Coleman slept,
become the source that makes
the river flow, and then the sea
beyond. Live in this place
as you were meant to and then,
surprised by your abilities,
become the ancestor of it all,
the quiet, robust, and blessed Saint
that your future happiness
will always remember.

Coleman's Bed is a poem that I felt spoke directly to my own personality type. I had been studying the Enneagram, an ancient tool for understanding human behavior by bringing into focus one's individual personality patterns of habitual behavior. The Enneagram map points to the underlying true Essence of each of nine core personality types, each type given a neutral number One to Nine. Scholars of this work refer to these as 'essential qualities.' They are the capacities for real integrity, love, authenticity, creativity, understanding, guidance, joy, power, and serenity. The Enneagram illustrates how we get caught in habitual patterns of behavior stemming from our genetic inheritance impacted by early life experiences, what we name the personality, all in an unconscious attempt to come back and recreate the unique quality of our being, our essential quality— our true nature.

As dominant in the Personality Type Two called the 'Helper,' I lived in the territory of giving and hopefully receiving appreciation and love. As I explored the rich material I was being taught and began to take a hard look at my own behavior I was beginning to see how extreme my efforts had become to assure myself that I was indeed lovable. I was literally caught on a daily spinning wheel of giving, helping, giving, helping and more giving to others; and it never felt like enough. My family medicine practice consumed my energy both physically and emotionally and what was left over went directly to my family and friends. I had become known among my friends as the woman always dutifully ready to rescue someone in need.

Only now was I beginning to see the price I'd paid. The notion of attending to myself — oh yes I was fine with getting nice haircuts and my toenails painted — but really tending to my own emotional and spiritual needs seemed like foreign territory. Somehow all of my attention was directed outward toward the needs of others, never toward myself.

These habits I could now see, often painfully so, were really my attempts to convince myself that I was indeed deserving of value and love. The Enneagram pointed to my essential self — that of being loved and loving without having to *do* anything — but I didn't believe it. I had studied and read lots about this, yet I hadn't really gotten it, so to speak. The idea of being alone with myself and letting go of all the things I wanted at that moment to do for others was unfathomable. The pull away from myself and toward the other, like a magnetic force, was powerful. It was this poem, David Whyte's articulation of the depth of my soul that woke me up. Now I *got* it. It directed me to what was to become, in the ensuing years, my salvation.

...apprentice
yourself to yourself,
begin to welcome back
all you have sent away, be a new annunciation,
make yourself a door through which
to be hospitable, even to the stranger in you.

and above all, be alone with it all,
a hiving off, a corner of silence
amidst the noise, refuse to talk,
even to yourself, and stay in this place
until the current of the story
is strong enough to float you out.

That first remarkable day and night by the sea was the beginning of a transformative process that would shift my perspective and open me to my deeper Essence and change my life. My marriage would crumble and reform with honesty and strength; I would go to the Lakes in the north of England and live one winter by myself, walking the paths of the great romantic poets and for the first time know myself; and I would engage my work with a new wholehearted steadfastness which would blossom and give me a foundation of settledness. I would no longer be in a muddle. It all began with a poem.

By selecting poems that reflect the constellation of gifts, habits, fears, and desires of a personality type, — the highs and the lows — I wish to offer you the reader an enjoyable and enriching way to both explore your own gifts and challenges, as well as those of 'the other.' It is my hope that you, aided with the piercing light of poetry, will grow to recognize, understand, and appreciate the struggle and path in both yourself and others. Knowing yourself, understanding the other and bringing compassion to both is a healing salve for humanity.

As you read a particular poem a feeling may be evoked which may seem so familiar that it makes your body tingle in resonance, while others may seem strange yet vaguely familiar. Some poems may jolt awake something long asleep, while others plunge you into an awareness of something about yourself you'd rather not see. These will necessitate a healthy dose of self-compassion along the way. While it is validating and fun to contemplate our higher qualities and see ourselves at our personal best, it is never easy to look hard and long at our crusty parts; yet this is where we often find the greatest opportunity for personal growth. I invite you to explore a variety of poems, each chosen to help you to mine the depths of a particular Personality type. Perhaps one will, like one did for me, change your life.

Part I

Chapter 1 On Poetry and The Enneagram

On Poetry

A poem is *a piece of concentrated power,* so wrote twentieth century anthologist and poet Louis Untermeyer.[1] Words finely chosen, placed in a precise pattern, infused with a felt rhythm pulsing from the page, make an impact.

That words have this power and impact, few would deny. Great leaders and great lovers know it, as do the most creative of marketing agents. Robert Frost's *Two roads diverged in a yellow wood...* brings us immediately to the demand of a choice to be made, or from the intensity of John Keat's *Ode on Melancholy* I know of no better evocation of the oppression of sunken mood — *the melancholy fit shall fall sudden from heaven like a weeping cloud, that fosters the droop headed flowers all...,* likewise great leaders can move nations as Churchill did with his simple words *never was so much owed by so many to so few,* and the US Army's *Be all that you can be* has no shelf life. Definitions and usage may change over time, but the deceptively simple choice of word, order, and rhythm can create magic. If we have forgotten, we now remember; if we are frightened we find courage; if our hearts have shattered, they now reform.

Plato said that poetry comes closer to vital truth than history. By *springing into shaking and passionate life* as modern poet Mary Oliver writes[2], poetry hits us not only in our thinking mind, but in our feeling heart, and deeply down in our instinctive gut. While Nike

---

[1] *The Treasury of Great Poems, Louis Untermeyer 1942* Simon & Schuster, Preface xlviii

[2] *A Poetry Handbook*, Mary Oliver 1994, Harcourt, Inc.

may use words to sell us a pair of running shoes, the poet uses words to wake us up, be it to a delightful image or a deeply known truth about ourselves.

Poetry, while often viewed as somehow highly intellectual and inaccessible to the everyday person, is in fact a part of our daily language of life, permeating and coloring the most ordinary of days, for we don't just say it's raining, but it's raining *cats and dogs;* we enjoy *honey-dew* melon, the name inspired by Coleridge's lines *For he on honey-dew hath fed and drunk the milk of Paradise;* and when we accelerate in our new sports car we don't simply drive but we *eat up* the road. Imagery abounds.

Keats called poetry *a remembrance;* Faust *a distillation;* Wordsworth *a preservation of everything which humanity loves, works for, and hopes to maintain.* A poem can awaken our intellect as it stirs our emotions and inspires our higher self. It can impact our mind, belly, and heart with the mere choice of a word; surprise of a phrase; beat of a long forgotten primal rhythm. By doing so a poem can invite the reader— in fact it must invite the reader if it is a good poem — to a new awareness acutely felt in his deepest place of knowing. A poem can touch the soul.

~ ~ ~

On the Enneagram

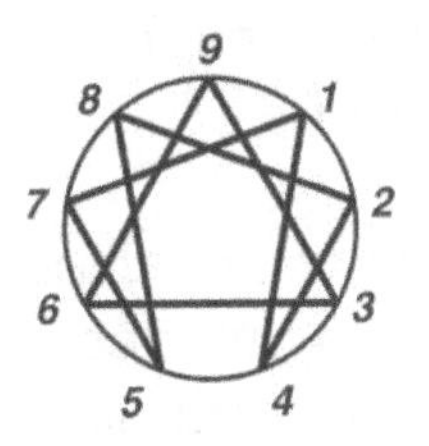

The Enneagram, as an ancient tool melded with modern psychology for understanding human behavior, is also a *distillation.* The Enneagram symbol itself has ancient roots and what is known of its history suggests that from its inception it was a map — a guide for a human being to look at his or herself, see what is so hard to see, and anticipate how one loses his or her way. The symbol is dynamic: a circle whose perimeter has nine numbered points each representing a distinct personality type and each connected through lines of flow to two other personality types. Each line points toward or away from a potential and predictable challenge or strength inherent in that linked type.

As a description of the human condition, how we are all the same yet uniquely different, the Enneagram provides a guide to study where our attention goes and how it affects all the relationships in our lives. By bringing curiosity, an open mind as well as a compassionate heart, we can inquire into 'how we tick' and with this process discover many things about our own capacities and capabilities. The knowledge and insights broaden our horizons and loosen the constrictions keeping us stuck as they hold us back from fulfillment in every aspect of our lives.

Through observation of human behavior across millennia these nine types have been identified and given names by scholars to reflect the gift each particular personality brings out into the world. I have chosen the names given to the nine types by Don Riso and Russ Hudson[3] because they represent the gift which each type can potentially bring out into the world.

Below are thumbnail sketches of the nine personality types as described on the map of the Enneagram. Each type has:

- **An Essential Quality**
- **A Focus of Attention**
- **A Blindspot**
- **A Doorway**

Our **Essential Quality** is that natural gift that we are born with, that which is bred in the bone. The variety of gifts sprinkled amongst we human beings is dazzling, if only we could all use them at our personal best. Each type exhibits a specific **Focus of Attention**. This is where, often unconsciously, our energy is drawn as we live life. This focus of attention can deteriorate into a driving emotional energy which pulls us away from our own groundedness. This is our **Blindspot.** By not seeing this in ourselves, by being blind to it, we tend to operate like mechanical toys, doing the same things over and over again and remaining stuck in the same patterns. The good news is that for each of us there is a specific **Doorway** existing as an invitation toward coming back to our true Essence, our true gifts by consciously seeing where we have been in the dark, so to speak, and shining light on a new path. By focusing on these core features of each Enneagram temperament a useful snapshot materializes the way a photo taken emerges

[3] *Wisdom of the Enneagram, Don Richard Riso and Russ Hudson, Bantam Books, 1999*

from the developing fluid in a dark room. We are all so often in our own dark rooms in need of some help to *see* with new clarity what we are all about.

For each type I've given examples of famous individuals who, despite his or her flaws, personify the qualities of Essence he or she shares with the world.

The nine types are divided up into three triads representing the three Centers of Intelligence all humans possess. It is from these Intelligences, that of our Instinctual Gut Center, Our Feeling Heart Center, and our Thinking Head Center that we have the tools to negotiate life. These three core intelligences evolved over millions of years, first with the reptilian brain supplying the most instinctive and basic of bodily physiological needs - a beating heart circulating blood and the breath to feed that circulation. Next came the Limbic part of the brain coding for emotion creating the ability to feel about and care for another animal which are crucial for a mammal's survival. Most recently across the millennia of human evolution the Cerebral Cortex developed allowing humans to think, weigh, and judge choices, thereby providing the means to integrate all three intelligences and reflect upon his or her existence.

Each type falling within a particular triad, although possessing from birth all three intelligences, is most sensitive to that center's particular intelligence and most challenged around managing that center's primary energy. Each type deals with a powerful emotion stemming from that center. The Body Types must manage the instinctual energy of anger; the Heart Types the emotional grip of shame; and the Head Types the buzzing energy of anxiety. We will see how this plays out in human behavior as we explore each type in the chapters ahead. For now, here they are in a nutshell.

The Body (Instinctive) Triad - *seeking Autonomy & Respect*

• Type 8 the Challenger

- **Essential Quality:** Strength and Courage
- **Focus of Attention:** Being strong and in control
- **Blindspot:** Control & Dominance
- **Doorway:** Embracing vulnerability

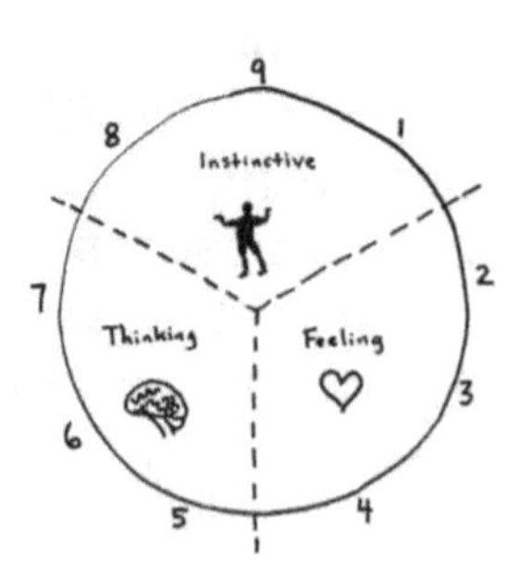

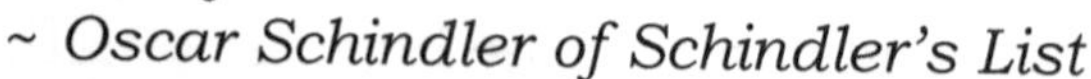

~ *Oscar Schindler of Schindler's List*
~ *St. Mother Teresa*
~ *Martin Luther King, Jr.*

• Type 9 the Peacemaker

- **Essential Quality:** Unity and Wholeness
- **Focus of Attention:** Creating harmony and comfort
- **Blindspot:** Peace of mind at any cost
- **Doorway:** Engagement with Life

~ *Abraham Lincoln*
~ *Ringo Starr*
~ *Whoopi Goldberg*

• Type 1 the Reformer

- **Essential Quality:** Goodness and Serenity
- **Focus of Attention:** Making things right with reason

- **Blindspot:** Resentment and dissatisfaction with the world
- **Doorway:** Laying down the burden of trying to make life perfect

~ *Nelson Mandela*
~ *Mahatma Ghandi*
~ *Mary Poppins*

The Heart (Feeling) Triad - *seeking Attention & Validation*

• Type 2 the Helper

- **Essential Quality:** Unconditional Love and Sweetness
- **Focus of Attention:** Relationships, reaching out to others
- **Blindspot:** Pride in believing I do not need help
- **Doorway:** Attending to my own needs and acknowledging my own suffering

~ *Albert Schweitzer*
~ *Eleanor Roosevelt*
~ *Jane in Jane Austen's Pride and Prejudice*

• Type 3 the Achiever

- **Essential Quality:** Real Value and Authenticity
- **Focus of Attention:** Winning approval by being successful and reaching goals
- **Blindspot:** Vanity in my attempt to make my ego feel valuable
- **Doorway:** Letting go of deceiving myself and others in order to be the best

~ *Oprah Winfrey*
~ *Deepak Chopra*
~ *Christopher Reeves*

• Type 4 the Individualist

- **Essential Quality:** True Identity and Depth
- **Focus of Attention:** Directed Inward toward feelings as I look for what's missing
- **Blindspot:** Envy for what I feel is missing, failing to notice ordinary blessings in life
- **Doorway:** Finding the extraordinary in the ordinary and in myself

~ *Peter Tchaikovsky*
~ *Rainer Maria Rilke*
~ *Frieda Kahlo*

The Head (Thinking) Triad - *seeking Security & Guidance*

• Type 5 the Investigator

- **Essential Quality:** Real Knowing and Clarity
- **Focus of Attention:** Analyzing how things work, exploring Ideas
- **Blindspot:** Withholding Energy and Resources Fearing I won't be able to Cope
- **Doorway:** Trusting contact with the world and reaching out to others with my gifts

~ Albert Einstein
~ Georgia O'Keefe
~ Charles Darwin

• Type 6 the Loyal Skeptic

- **Essential Quality:** Real Guidance and Will
- **Focus of Attention:** Security, looking for what could go wrong
- **Blindspot:** Anxiety and doubt as I lack faith in myself, others, the future, and life itself
- **Doorway:** Letting go of believing I have to foresee every possible problem

~ *Moses*
~ *Robert F. Kennedy*
~ *Bruce Springsteen*

• Type 7 the Enthusiast

- **Essential Quality:** Real Joy and Freedom
- **Focus of Attention:** Possibility! Looking for what's next.
- **Blindspot:** Insatiably 'filling myself up' with experiences as I fear inner emptiness
- **Doorway:** Allowing in the contentment that maybe I already have enough

~ *Sir Elton John*
~ *Amelia Earhart*
~ *Wolfgang Amadeus Mozart*

In each of these distinct personalities we can see behaviors which show up in predictable ways, each stemming from the core motivations, fears, and instinctual drives of that type. These form the essence of the *who* of who we are, or at least how we see who we are.

Bringing Poetry and the Enneagram Together

Just as study of the Enneagram can lead us to a new understanding of ourselves, so too can imbibing a perfectly crafted poem bring us into contact with our deepest gifts and our thorny flaws: the impact we make in the world or our retreat from it; the way we engage love deeply, or in contrast close down our hearts; the manner in which we cope with adversity in life or flee from it.

How we, as unique individuals *be*, that is, fit into this cosmic scheme is, and has been, the compelling question our species has pondered since the dawn of time. Biblical Job asked it as did Shakespeare's Hamlet and, in our own era of expanding scientific knowledge, so too do particle physicists.

These core human concerns permeate both our work with the Enneagram and our engagement with fine poetry. The Enneagram is a tool for bringing order out of the stunning complexity of human behavior; the great poem likewise brings order out of the chaos of our thoughts, and feelings, and biologic drives. Czeslaw Milosz, towering Twentieth century poet, said this of poetry's capacity to help us see once again with a kind of beginner's mind: *In a way poetry is an attempt to break through the density of reality into a zone where the simplest things are again as fresh as if they were being seen by a child.*

Both the Enneagram and good poetry offer us the opportunity to deepen and illuminate our place in the grand scheme of things. They each shed light onto the dynamics of the nine core temperaments which comprise humanity. I see the Enneagram as a brilliant noon sun shining light into every nook and cranny of human behavior while poetry is a subtler rosy first dawn glow or the gloaming's deepening shades of night.

The Enneagram, by describing the totality of being human, brings awareness to our strengths as well as our weaknesses. It elucidates how each personality looks out into the world with its own unique perspective, utilizing behaviors most easily accessible to that individual. But, and this is an essential *but,* we each have all nine of these capacities within us despite the genetic fact that we are neuro-physiologically designed to call most easily upon specific tools, just as someone with a musical gift might express an emotion through song and a painter through his or her art. For example, Albert Einstein did indeed possess an extraordinary gift for bringing abstract ideas and patterns together (the great strength of the Type Five temperament), but we all, regardless of personality type, still have the capacity to contemplate an idea.

In the pages that follow I've gathered a variety of poems, one of which may gently remind us of a forgotten capacity or another startle us awake into seeing a long neglected truth about ourselves. Likewise, there are poems to remind us of success and poems to alert us to lurking pitfalls. Some may elicit a tear, others a hearty laugh. These selections are all meant to offer a richer tapestry within which to wrap our human experience.

Reading good poetry is not meant to be a brainy contest in puzzle interpretation, but an invitation to a new experience. Poet Laureate Billy Collins put it this way in his marvelous poem written to his students, instructing them in how to approach a new poem—and how *not* to.

INTRODUCTION TO POETRY

I ask them to take a poem
and hold it up to the light
like a color slide

or press an ear against its hive.

I say drop a mouse into a poem
and watch him probe his way out,

or walk inside the poem's room
and feel the walls for a light switch.

I want them to waterski
across the surface of a poem
waving at the author's name on the shore.

But all they want to do
is tie the poem to a chair with rope
and torture a confession out of it.

They begin beating it with a hose
to find out what it really means.

Neither do I wish you to 'torture a confession' out of any of the poems in this collection but only to hopefully allow each to guide you to do, for you, what Louis Untermeyer said:

The poem must make the reader see with a new acuteness and feel with a new awareness. [4]

---

[4] *A Treasury of Great Poems*, Louis Untermeyer 1942, Simon & Schuster, Preface xlix

As a thirteen year old girl I was given a book of Robert Frost poems with an inscription to pay particular attention to the poem *The Road Not Taken.* I read that poem over and over and did indeed allow myself to waterski across its surface. It was in my mind as I made the decision to run away from home at fifteen; it was in my mind when I looked back on a decision to let another choose my fate — pursuing the study of medicine instead of my beloved literature; and when I, years later, stepped away from something I did not love.

Yes, a poem can make the reader, this reader, see with a new acuteness and with this seeing choose a road not taken.

In spite of things silently gone out of mind, and things violently destroyed, the poet binds together by passion and knowledge the vast empire of human society as it is spread over the whole earth and over all time.
~ William Wordsworth

Chapter 2 Nine Parts of the Whole

Most of our lives we are busy being the particular flavor of our personality. How often do we say something along the lines of "I can't sit and quiet my mind because I'm a doer, not a contemplator," or "I can't go forward until I have *all* the data, my mind just doesn't work that way" — or many other versions of what we can't do because 'that's not how we operate.' Need we always be the same edition of ourselves?

In truth we have many capacities from which to draw, but like a nine tiered tool chest where we keep our most familiar and oft used tools in the top drawer and the least in the bottom, so too from day to day do we tend to pull out our most habitual behaviors. These behavioral habits are strong and because we have been using them, often unconsciously, for our entire lives they are difficult to see. We might be in the habit of always saying yes when asked to do something or quite the opposite automatically saying no as we withdraw from demands. We may routinely doubt most every opportunity that comes our way, holding back or we may, again just the opposite, charge full speed ahead without much reflection. It can be mortifying to notice just how often we act in the same patterns of behavior using our long familiar tools. But what about those others tools?

The Enneagram is a description of the whole of human capacity. It helps us to focus the quality of our attention on both what comes naturally and what does not. With its map of the nine distinct domains of 'standard operating procedure' — our automatic habitual patterns of behavior — and the many nuances to each, we have a lens through which to explore the whys and hows of human behavior. We can see both our innate qualities, like serenity or clarity alongside all the efforts we make to create that quality as if we didn't already have it. Perhaps we will work very hard collecting every piece of data we can find to gain clarity when what proves most effective is ceasing the search, quieting our mind, and opening up to revelations. This indeed is how all great discoveries have been made from Plato to Einstein.

The opportunity, the fun of the exploration of the entire circle is like that of a treasure hunt. The map lures us to the discovery of unexpected capacities within our own being. It is like our whole being is a mansion and until now we've lived in only a room or two. What treasures lie behind all those closed doors.

The Enneagram shows us nine points of view, nine value systems, and nine ways of being in the world. Yet we are so often stuck in our own perspective. It is helpful to have a way to nudge us into glimpses of other possibilities, open those doors previously hidden from our view, and see what's inside. Ezra Pound said this about poetry as a means to assist us in this search:

"Poetry is not greatly concerned with what a man thinks, but with what
is so embedded in his nature that it never occurs to him to question it;
not a matter of which idea he holds, but of the depth at which he holds it."

Poetry is an invitation to mine these 'embedded' parts of our nature. As T. S. Eliot said, "Poetry is not the assertion that something is true, but the making of that truth more fully real to us."

Here are some poems that invite us into the exploration. The treasure chest is full of gems if we know where to look.

EPISTLE II

Alexander Pope (1688-1744)

Know then thyself, presume not God to scan;
The proper study of Mankind is Man.
Plac'd on this isthmus of a middle state,
A Being darkly wise, and rudely great:
With too much knowledge for the Skeptic side,
With too much weakness for the Stoic's pride,
He hangs between; in doubt to act, or rest;
In doubt to deem himself a God, or Beast;
In doubt his Mind or Body to prefer;
Born but to die, and reas'ning but to err;
Alike in ignorance, his reason such,
Whether he thinks too little, or too much:
Chaos of Thought and Passion, all confused;
Still by himself abus'd, or disabused;
Created half to rise, and half to fall;
Great lord of all things, yet a prey to all;
Sole judge of Truth, in endless Error hurl'd:
The glory, jest, and riddle of the world!
Go, wond'rous creature! mount where Science guides,
Go, measure earth, weigh air, and state the tides;
Instruct the planets in what orbs to run,
Correct old Time, and regulate the Sun.

In this excerpt from *An Essay on Man* learned English poet Alexander Pope wrote: *it is all laid out: this wonderful, chaotic, mixture of all that we are.* As we look at the parts of the whole we have a powerful map and approach for Pope's dictum *The proper study of Mankind is Man.* He touches upon the challenges of our differing gifts; too much of what we most possess, or too little. With razor sharp wit he ends by mocking our hubris to think that we can *Correct old Time, and regulate the Sun.* Pope invites us to the *proper study,* an invitation to examine ourselves so that we might discover that part *darkly wise and rudely great.*

We shall examine within the structure of each personality type what Pope describes as *Chaos of Thought and Passion, all confused,* and look to poetry for help in 'sorting' ourselves, as the Brits would say.

With *plac'd on this isthmus of a middle state* Pope tips his hat to Dante who opened his famous Inferno with the line 'Midway in our life's journey, I went astray from the straight road and woke to find myself alone in a dark wood.' So often it only comes with living and some degree of maturity that we can enter this 'dark wood' and have the means to reflect back on our life. Pope's *A Being darkly wise, and rudely great* points us to our Essential Quality, a quality we may have lost touch with. He reminds us of our depth.

The first time I read this poem I was struck with how accurately this Seventeenth Century poet named some of man's most noticeable habits all still so alive and present in our Twenty-first century:

— *He hangs between; in doubt to act, or rest*; — our habit to jostle back and forth between full-of-doubt inaction and incessant action

— *Whether he thinks too little, or too much* — our tendency to overthink and under think, attempting to find our way
— *Created half to rise, and half to fall* — Our inflating self rising, rising as our deflating self falls, and falls
—*Sole judge of Truth, in endless Error hurl'd* — our daily dilemma of desire for righteousness amidst the terror of error
— *Chaos of Thought and Passion, all confused* — the dilemma for all of us as our emotions hijack our reason

We see in this poem the story of the Types — the habits of personality. As we approach the poems ahead I hope to provide a framework for seeing these parts in all of us. Pope starts us off with a bold stroke as he articulates for us and deepens the meaning of the importance of *The proper study of Mankind is Man,* which is precisely, in my view, the purpose of the Enneagram.

~ ~ ~

The invitation to gaze upon all the parts of ourselves need not be some sort of dull chore or labored inventory of personality, but quite the contrary as an exploration filled with flavor—something to taste and savor. My wish for you is to let yourself *taste* a poem and in so doing savor the beauty of all the Types.

BLACKBERRY EATING
Galway Kinnell (1927-2014)

I love to go out in late September
among the fat, overripe, icy, blackberries
to eat blackberries for breakfast,
the stalks very prickly, a penalty
they earn for the black art
of blackberry-making; and as I stand among them
lifting the stalks to my mouth, the ripest berries
fall almost unbidden on the tongue,
as words sometimes do, certain peculiar words
like *strengths* or *squinched,*
many-lettered, one-syllabled lumps,
which I squeeze, squinch open, and splurge well
in the silent, startled, icy, black language
of blackberry-eating in late September.

In *Blackberry Eating,* an evocative poem by New England poet and Pulitzer prize winner Galway Kinnell we are invited to savor along with the poet. Kinnell was a man of many interests and talents: poet, essayist, children's author, Naval officer, world traveler, Civil Rights activist, Vietnam War critic, and Poet Laureate of the state of Vermont. Literary critic Liz Rosenberg of the Boston Globe said that he was a poet who 'can flesh out music, raise the spirits and break the heart.' He gives us here, in this concise scene, literally a taste of the fun of discovery and an invitation to s*queeze and squinch open and splurge well* on the lush language of poetry and all that it can awaken in us.

It is in this spirit that we can begin the deep dive into the understanding of our Type. We might say the nine points on the Enneagram map represent nine strong flavors, each with many possible nuances, and we are invited to taste them all.

~ ~ ~

The theme of Unity, everything and everyone part of the whole, is central to any sort of spiritual, emotional, or mindful work as we explore our being and our place in the cosmos. The image of the Mandala comes to mind — a circle of the whole universe with the human consciousness, the soul at its center. The whole is dynamic as it unfolds according to an intelligent pattern. We unfold at its center as an integral part, being influenced by everything and also influencing everything. Nothing is separate or static.

As we study the Types and taste them through the medium of poetry we can feel this unity, how we are all in this together. The more that the habitual habits of each type relax, the more we can begin to feel the connection. Barriers break down as we come together in our common humanity.

Mary Oliver gives us a memorable image of this unity in *Poem of The One World.* Oliver is a mistress of imagery, crafting her poems so that they might invite us into *a place to enter, and in which to feel.* She described the writing of her deceptively simple poems in this way: "It takes about seventy hours to drag a poem into the light."

POEM OF THE ONE WORLD

This morning
the beautiful white heron
was floating along above the water
and then into the sky of this
the one world
we all belong to

where everything
sooner or later
is a part of everything else

which thought made me feel
for a little while
quite beautiful myself

It is this inner beauty emanating from each of us that the Enneagram points to. For me there is no finer benefit of this study than that of remembering and resonating with this deeper beauty.

~ ~ ~

As we explore the nine personality perspectives looking out into the world we will notice our own habitual behaviors. It is helpful to be reminded of what these behaviors, so automatic to us that we barely notice we are doing them, look like — call it a forewarning of sorts; for if we can't see it (whatever the behavior may be) and bring it into our awareness, we have no hope at all of acting upon it. Being reminded of all the ways we lose track of our best selves is useful for our work, as Alexander Pope in the previous poem reminded us: *The proper study of Mankind is Man.*

Nobel Prize winning Polish poet Wislawa Szymborska (1923-2012) offers us in her *A Contribution to Statistics* a kind of grocery list of human frailty. Szymborska had a keen eye and a piercing ability to hone in on behavior. I love the way she names a habit of personality like being *righteous* — the habitual effort of the personality of the Type One individual and then follows with the Type One's Essential Quality, that of being *righteous with understanding*. She gives us a wonderful example of the authentic quality alongside the ersatz one. And then there is *doubting every step*, the territory of the Type Six. We'll have to wait until the chapter on Type Six to see examples of the Six's Essential Quality, Trust.

In these deceptively simple lines I ask you, where do you fit in 'worthy of compassion?'

A CONTRIBUTION TO STATISTICS

Out of a hundred people

those who always know better
—fifty-two,

doubting every step
—nearly all the rest,

glad to lend a hand
if it doesn't take too long
—as high as forty-nine.

always good
because they can't be otherwise
—four, well maybe five,

able to admire without envy
—eighteen,

suffering illusions
induced by fleeting youth
—sixty, give or take a few,

not to be taken lightly
—forty and four,

living in constant fear

of someone or something
—seventy-seven,

capable of happiness
—twenty-something tops,

harmless singly,
savage in crowds
—half, at least,

cruel
when forced by circumstances
—better not to know
even ballpark figures

wise after the fact
—just a couple more
than wise before it,

taking only things from life
—thirty
(I wish I were wrong,)

hunched in pain,
no flashlight in the dark
—eighty-three
sooner or later,

righteous
—thirty-five, which is a lot,

righteous
and understanding
—three

worthy of compassion
—ninety-nine,

mortal

—a hundred out of a hundred.
Thus far this figure still remains unchanged.

~ ~ ~

As we open our minds to self-examination, observing our own habits and behaviors as well as those of others, there will be inevitable times when an inner voice screams "Stop! — I don't want to see just how alike I am to that woman who just did that or the man who actually said that! I'm not like that at all — no, indeed — stop!" We put up a wall, speaking metaphorically, between our own personality and that of the other.

It can be so tempting to stay snugly in our own well defined image, our own custom fashioned identity box with stout fancy sides. Our walls of rigid self image provide us with the illusion of protection — we are who we are, dang it, and nobody is going to tell us otherwise! The invitation is to let the walls crumble, at least a bit and gaze openly through the gaps to the other side, all the time pondering what we might learn about ourselves. The nine personality types are points within a spectrum, not walled off fortresses to defend. We need not be addicted to our walls, but find that light switch Billy Collins in his 'Introduction to Poetry' invited us to flip on, and look about.

Robert Frost (1874-1963), perhaps our finest American poet alongside Walt Whitman, reflects upon *Something there is that doesn't love a wall,* in his early poem *Mending Wall.* A core piece of Enneagram work is the awareness of how we in so many ways live walled off in our own rigid self conceptions.

Frost begins his poem with syntax that busts us out of our comfortable way of hearing a phrase. Compare *For some reason some people don't love walls* to *Something there is that doesn't love a wall* and feel the jolt demanding us to stop, read that again, take it in and give it some deeper thought. Already we are more curious and alert to the story that follows.

Frost, a New England farmer himself, sets up a dialogue between two neighbors whose fields meet at a stone wall in need of repair. On one side of the wall is Frost asking why do we need to rebuild it when neither of us have any cows at risk of escaping to eat each others apples. He is curious and in the mood to press his questions. Feel his open, non-constricted approach to this little encounter. His farmer neighbor is, on the other hand, rigid in his response with his long conditioned response *Good fences make good neighbors.*

And still Frost presses him, *Why?* as he reflects to us the reader that he's feeling *spring is the mischief in me.* He knows darn well the response he'll get. But he can't give up trying as he invites the farmer to a little fantasy — perhaps it is Elves who are responsible. After all it is a mystery, this deep question. A no starter again, his musing falling on stone ears.

The farmer *like an old-stone savage armed* is the very image of our habits stretching back through time, set in stone and as immovable as long as we choose to *move in darkness,* clinging to our past conditioning and invulnerable to the possibilities of the present, for after all there are no cows.

Frost invites us to ponder along with him, stepping out of the darkness and out from behind old beliefs and platitudes, and touch upon our Essence, our True Nature, that *Something is that doesn't love a wall.*

MENDING WALL

from *North of Boston, 1914*

Something there is that doesn't love a wall,
That sends the frozen-ground-swell under it
And spills the upper boulders in the sun,
And makes gaps even two can pass abreast.
The work of hunters is another thing:
I have come after them and made repair
Where they have left not one stone on a stone,
But they would have the rabbit out of hiding,
To please the yelping dogs. The gaps I mean,
No one has seen them made or heard them made,
But at spring mending-time we find them there.
I let my neighbor know beyond the hill;
And on a day we meet to walk the line
And set the wall between us once again.
We keep the wall between us as we go.
To each the boulders that have fallen to each.
And some are loaves and some so nearly balls
We have to use a spell to make them balance:
"Stay where you are until our backs are turned!"
We wear our fingers rough with handling them.
Oh, just another kind of outdoor game,
One on a side. It comes to little more:
There where it is we do not need the wall:
He is all pine and I am apple orchard.
My apple trees will never get across
And eat the cones under his pines, I tell him.
He only says, "Good fences make good neighbors."
Spring is the mischief in me, and I wonder
If I could put a notion in his head:
"*Why* do they make good neighbors? Isn't it
Where there are cows? But here there are no cows.
Before I built a wall I'd ask to know
What I was walling in or walling out,
And to whom I was like to give offense.

Something there is that doesn't love a wall,
that wants it down." I could say "Elves" to him,
But it's not elves exactly, and I'd rather
He said it for himself. I see him there,
Bringing a stone grasped firmly by the top
In each hand, like an old-stone savage armed.
He moves in darkness as it seems to me,
Not of woods only and the shade of trees.
He will not go behind his father's saying,
And he likes having thought of it so well
He says again, "Good fences make good neighbors."

~ ~ ~

It is fitting to end this chapter with a poem encouraging the care of the Essence of our Being, our True Nature. John Collop (1625-1700) was a Seventeenth Century metaphysical poet, a physician by profession, and a liberal who wrote pleas for religious tolerance — a dangerous attitude in his day. While his is not an everyday name even for those familiar with the literature of this era, Collop still deserves notice for this inspiring call to us to return the fire (our unique gift) from which *Heaven gave the spark.*

As we explore the Nine temperaments we will be looking at the great gift of each. We all have, with self-knowledge and compassion, the opportunity for growth, expansion and the means to thrive. Our soul is the seat of that fire which can grow from our creative spark — no matter our personality type.

Listen to Collop's invocation of our deepest capacity and the challenge to bring back to our world the *fire* that lies within such a capacity. He warns us that sin (where we will all at some time certainly 'miss the mark') needn't quench it and in fact we can sweep our house and *find the penny* which we lost— a reference to the parable Jesus tells in the Gospel of

Luke in which the coin represents the lost awareness of our True Nature's deeper calling. Both the Enneagram and fine poems can assist us in 'finding the penny' though I would argue that what we find is far more valuable than the worth of a penny.

Collop pleads with us in his Seventeenth Century language to *spare no cost* — stay open and curious and do our Work paying attention to our soul's longing. Speak out in the voice of our highest self, for *When angels needs must speak, shall man be mute?*

TO THE SOUL

Dull soul aspire;
Thou art not earth. Mount higher!
Heaven gave the spark; to it return the fire.

Let sin ne'er quench
Thy high-flamed spirit hence;
To earth the heat, to heaven the flame dispense!

Rejoice! Rejoice!
turn, turn, each part a voice;
While to the heart-strings' tune ye all rejoice.

The house is swept
Which sin so long foul kept;
The penny's found for which the loser wept.

And purged with tears,
God's image reappears.
The penny truly shows whose stamp it bears.

The sheep long lost,
Sin's wilderness oft crossed,

Is found, regained, returned. Spare, spare no cost!

'Tis heaven's own suit;
Hark how it woos you to't.
When angels needs must speak, shall man be mute?

~ ~ ~

Part II
Three Groups of Three
The Social Styles

Three Groups of Three
The Social Styles

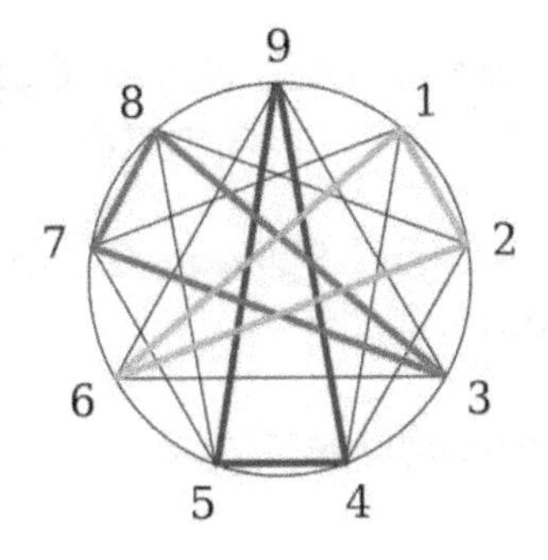

In the chapters that follow you will find explorations of the nine distinct personality types presented in groups of three. Each exploration is through the lens of a specific poem that in some way illuminates something worth seeing about that type's unique perspective and way of interacting in life.

The Enneagram is inherently triadic in nature. That is, things can be grouped into threes from a variety of perspectives. Each of these perspectives helps to understand more deeply the core coping strategies of different personalities. One of these Triads, *The Social Styles* or *Hornevians* is based upon how one copes with the stress of interpersonal relationships. The questions around which these types are clustered are: "How do I get my needs met?" and "In social situations, how do I feel most comfortable and act as I attempt to address my needs?"

These triads are modeled and named after the work of the brilliant psychiatrist Karen Horney, M.D. (1885-1952) who was a student of Sigmund Freud. Horney described how different personalities meet anticipated inner conflict by moving their energy either *toward, against, or away from* another.

The Social Style Core Question: *"How do I get my specific need met?*

Dutiful Types - I move toward others as I attempt to earn it

Assertive Types - I move against others as I demand it

Withdrawn Types - I withdraw and pull back inward as I attempt to figure it out

The Dutiful or Compliant Types **(One, Two, and Six)** all share a strong inner sense of obligation and responsibility. They often work in service oriented activities and due to their strong inner critics can have difficulty quieting their minds.

The Assertive or Initiating Types **(Three, Seven, and Eight)** all share a tendency toward expansive energy as they move out powerfully going after what they want. Often skilled at communicating directly and with assurance and intensity; however, this strategy can end by discounting the feelings of others as well as creating difficulty connecting with their own emotional feelings.

The Withdrawn or Contemplative Types **(Four, Five, and Nine)** all share a tendency to disengage from others in order to deal with their own needs. They may retreat into an inner world in order to avoid external demands. The challenge becomes how to stay in the present and connected with the reality of their own bodies as they disappear into their own mental considerings.

The Withdrawn Types

Nine Four Five

Hide not your Talents, they for Use were made, What's a Sun-Dial in the Shade!

~ Benjamin Franklin

Nine
The Peacemaker

The Type Nine sits at the apex of the Enneagram and in many ways the essential qualities of this temperament, those of real wholeness, unity, being and belonging, are essential qualities at the core of each of us, regardless of our personality type. The capacity to be wholly in the moment, wholly present, awake, and engaged and functioning as part of the whole of creation is the special domain of the Type Nine and is indeed necessary for all of us to thrive. Regardless of the lens through which each type looks out into life, be it the Challenger's focus on strength or the Investigator's on clarity of knowing, the need to be fully present in the moment is essential to achieve that true strength or clarity. Our engaged presence opens the gateway of receptivity.

This deep desire for belonging is joined with the Type Nine's highest value, that of tranquility. It is easy to see how one can 'fly above the turbulence' as Russ Hudson describes the Nine's avoidance of conflict in the service of maintaining that calm. The danger lies, as it always does within our greatest gifts, when we overdo it. A kind of reversal occurs and we can find ourselves so avoiding disharmony that we disengage and *go along to get along* in order to keep the peace. The doorway for growth and positive change for the Nine in us is staying with the experience, showing up for life and contributing our value in the service of all. Then we truly belong.

Essential Gifts

- Wholeness, Equanimity and Stability

Focus of Attention

- Creating harmony and feeling peaceful

At my Best

- I am easy-going, relaxed, accepting, supportive, and stable
- I can see all sides of a situation and consider them fairly

As I lose contact with my Essential Self

- I go along with others denying my own desires to avoid conflict
- I may become stubborn, complacent, and lose myself in routine habits

When I've lost contact with my True Nature

- I tune others out and become passive aggressive
- I can become depressed, neglectful, and listless

Doorway to Growth

- Engagement with life

It is nothing to die; it is
frightening not to live.
~ Victor Hugo

Chapter 3 The Peacemaker

Ode: Intimations of Immortality
(lines from) William Wordsworth (1770-1850)
...
Our birth is but a sleep and a forgetting:
The Soul that rises with us, our life's Star,
Hath had elsewhere its setting,
And cometh from afar:
Not in entire forgetfulness,
And not in utter nakedness,
But trailing clouds of glory do we come
From God, who is our home:
Heaven lies about us in our infancy!

The capacity to be wholly in the moment, wholly present and engaged and functioning as part of all of creation — *Heaven lies about us in our infancy* — is the special domain of the Type Nine and an exemplar for us all. Regardless of the perspective of an individual, the need to be fully present in the moment is essential to achieve true clarity, feeling, and strength.

At the deepest level the Type Nine in us yearns for belonging, the experience of being a part of the 'all is one'. Wordsworth reassures us — *Our birth is but a sleep and a forgetting;* in other words we are part of the whole from the instant of our creation, even if we are not consciously aware of it. We already arrive *trailing clouds of glory.* We are alive, present, and part of the whole of creation from that first beating of our hearts.

Despite all the challenges of our modern world, when engaged and present the Type Nine experiences the interconnectedness of everything in existence. This capacity to be fully present in the moment is the basis for all self-knowledge and growth. Earlier in Wordsworth's contemplative *Ode* he calls himself back from mourning the loss of the innocent and fresh eyes of his boyhood to the life pulsing about him now, from shepherd boys to the joy of a May morning:

Ye, blessed Creatures, I have heard the call
Ye to each other make; I see
The heavens laugh with you in your jubilee;
My heart hath its coronal,
The fullness of your bliss, I feel—I feel it all.

Wordsworth feels it, feels it all. It is just this connectedness that lies deeply rooted in the Nine psyche.

Buddha in Glory
Rainer Maria Rilke (1875-1926) translated by Stephen Mitchell

Center of all centers, core of cores,
almond self-enclosed and growing sweet—
all this universe, to the furthest stars
and beyond them, is your flesh, your fruit.

Now you feel how nothing clings to you;
your vast shell reaches into endless space,
and there the rich, thick fluids rise and flow.
Illuminated in your infinite peace,

a billions stars go spinning through the night,
blazing high above your head.
But *in* you is the presence that
will be, when all the stars are dead.

German poet, playwright, novelist, and devoted correspondent (consider his remarkable *Letters to a Young Poet)* Rainer Maria Rilke was an immensely creative man who worked with fervor throughout his life, in spite of his ongoing painful and at times debilitating illnesses, to grow and develop all the parts of himself. Here in his beautiful description, so artfully translated by poet Stephen Mitchell, of this quality of wholeness Rilke uses the image of the Buddha, an image of a man who embodied a connectivity reaching *into endless space.*

When this part of us is most healthy and free we are functioning with deep receptivity, acceptance, and emotional stability and experience a deep connectivity to all. At the center of the Type Nine is the center of all centers, so to speak, or the *core of* cores as Rilke puts it. It is this sensibility that allows us to know our true being, our absolute presence in the grand scheme of things— the gift inherent in our creation. This is the very image of the Buddha: wholeness and stability connected to all.

Rilke lures us willingly into this realm of wholeness *of all centers* and assures us in his dazzling line: *a billions stars go spinning through the night,/blazing high above your head* that this presence is inextinguishable: *the presence that/will be, when all the stars are dead.*

Patience
Kay Ryan b. 1945

Patience is
wider than one
once envisioned,
with ribbons
of rivers
and distant
ranges and
tasks undertaken
and finished
with modest
relish by
natives in their
native dress.
Who would
have guessed
it possible
that waiting
is sustainable—
a place with
its own harvests.
Or that in
time's fullness
the diamond
of patience
couldn't be
distinguished
from the genuine
in brilliance
or hardness.

Pulitzer Prize winning American poet Kay Ryan writes a gorgeous tribute to the quality of Patience, a gift of the Type Nine. Note the physical form of the poem, like a long ribbon of words and images as she indeed describes Patience *with ribbons / of rivers / and distant/ ranges and / tasks undertaken/ and finished / with modest/ relish...* This modesty and easy flow of the Nine, never rushing, but flowing toward completion of a task, is created with a ribbon of words.

It is to this quality that so many are drawn. I recall working nights while in college in a Mexican restaurant called El Papagayo where I became expert at serving bubbling quesadillas and shimmering sopapillas. However; amidst all the lovely aromas and nourishing food, conflicts would arise between other servers, cooks, and most especially the managers. I would find myself getting so stirred up that I'd rant and rave before the corn chip warming drawer and spill out my frustrations to Maria, an older woman who'd worked in the cantina for many years. I realized that I always felt better when she was there. She would stand quietly, listen, softly smile, and offer some perspective that I'd not considered. She would never make me feel like my complaints did not have merit, yet she never fueled them as the prep cook often did. Maria, always the quiet presence, the safe harbor in the workplace storm— the lovely Type Nine in life.

Here Ryan uses not only words and images, but a visual and physical connection to the reader. I especially like the ending of this simple poem: how Ryan equates the solidity and strength and the precious quality of Patience with that of the brilliance and hardness of a diamond. It is this solid, sparkling quality that draws so many to a woman like Maria and helps us to seek this same in ourselves.

Baby Song
Tom Gunn (1929-2004)

From the private ease of Mother's womb
I fall into the lighted room.

Why don't they simply put me back
Where it is warm and wet and black?

But one thing follows on another.
Things were different inside Mother.

Padded and jolly I would ride
The perfect comfort of her inside.

They tuck me in a rustling bed
—I lie there, raging, small, and red.

In *Baby Song* written very much as one would write a nursery rhyme the speaker asks *Why don't they simply put me back/ Where it is warm and wet and black?* Feel the longing for the peaceful, quiet, undisturbed *private ease* of the womb which, once Gunn entered life, seemed to forever elude him.

Gunn lived a long and searching, albeit hard life. His mother, who was his muse, died a suicide when Gunn was just a teen. He lived and wrote of the 'The Great War' in his first book of poetry, as he struggled to find his peace, little knowing what 'great wars' were to follow.

For our poet, the result of being forced into this *lighted room* — this glaring and dangerous world, is the powerlessness of the newborn, tucked into a rustling bed and lying there *raging, small, and red.* So begins the build-up of ones defenses, ones way to survive this feelingly hostile world. This is the birth of the 'personality'— for we begin with rage and find a lulling in sleep. Gunn died in Berkeley, California at age 75 of a drug overdose, the ultimate lulling to sleep. The question he tacitly posed in this wee poem, is, I believe — how may we stay awake and survive.

Renaissance Man
Nayda Ivette Negron

Archetype of the Renaissance man
master painter who suffered from
chronic procrastination
only fifteen paintings
have been credited
as authentic
as your name
was not
signed!

How wonderful when I discovered this *nonet* (*novem* L. for nine), a form of verse composed of nine lines, the first line having nine syllables, the second eight... well, you get the idea. This poem was written as an entry into the 'Favorite Painter Contest' in a 2015 edition of the online poetry forum *Poetry Soup.* The idea of the Renaissance Man is that of the individual (and they weren't always men— think Julian of Norwich) fully developed in thinking, feeling, and doing. Aha! we have Leonardo Da Vinci: inventor, engineer, architect, astronomer, scientist, poet, artist, and creator of arguably the greatest treasures ever resulting from a paint saturated brush. Yet, so like our Type Nine individual who is searching and searching for just the right balance, the right combination having all parts considered, procrastination inevitably creeps in. Talk with any person dominant in this personality type and they'll admit to the most wonderful stories about procrastination. My own husband Frank excitedly showed me a book he found while browsing in the local bookstore: *The Art of Procrastination.* He is certainly in good company with Leonardo.

Mr. Meant-To

anonymous

Mr. Meant-To has a comrade
And his name is Didn't Do;
Have you ever chanced to meet them?
Did they ever call on you?

These two fellows live together
In the house of Never-Win,
And I'm told that it is haunted
By the ghost of Might-Have-Been.

Here is another poem about procrastination and its weighty cost. The procrastination happens because by avoiding the 'big' issues one is avoiding possible 'big' conflicts, so procrastinating, on say changing jobs or ending a relationship, is replaced with a myriad of tiny projects. A friend of mine told me that whenever he came up against these big-decision daunting tasks he would start to build another little birdhouse. He ended by having lots of nicely snug little chickadee homes but still no progress on the big issue. You might say it is a matter of little projects staving off the decision of the big ones.

A Way Around
Naomi Shihab Nye b. 1952

Argument
is a room I won't enter.
Some of us
Would circle a whole house
not to enter it.

If you want to talk like that,
try a tree.
A tree is patient.
Don't try me.

Avoidance of conflict can become a way of life for the Nine, so ingrained that one may appear frozen, stuck, and unmoving. Even with so few words, Nye creates in her clever miniature poem the stubborn energy of the avoidance of dis-ease, the dis-ease of confrontation. No way will this person engage in an argument, a contentious discussion. No way! It is *a room I won't enter.* The speaker advises the arguer to *try a tree.*

The choice of tree is a great metaphor for the Nine, standing immobile in the thick bark of a protective state, and refusing to engage. Yet all along there is the potential of flexibility, branches swaying in a breeze. The irony is that the Type Nine is arguably the most rooted and patient of all the types, yet when it comes to disturbing their own peace, they can be as immobile as a giant oak.

A STILL—VOLCANO—LIFE
Emily Dickinson (1830-1886)

A still—Volcano—Life—

That flickered in the night—
When it was dark enough to do
Without erasing sight—

A quiet—Earthquake Style—

Too subtle to suspect
By natures this side Naples—
The North cannot detect

The Solemn—Torrid—Symbol—
The lips that never lie—
Whose hissing Corals part—and shut—
And Cities—ooze away—

For an individual striving to maintain a peaceful calm, what could be worse than losing control and exploding in anger, the very epitome of ruining the peace. However; when one does finally express this anger it is a force which has been held under wraps for who knows how long and it tends to explode in a volcanic fashion. The image of molten lava building over years deep in the earth to eventually 'blow its top' in the form of an erupting Volcano is a perfect analogy for what happens with the Nine.

The reserved and shy New England poet Emily Dickinson 'The Belle of Amherst' captured the underlying energy at the core of the Type Nine personality: from the still and quiet *A still—volcano—Life*—to the *hissing Corals* which part and the result so that *Cities—ooze away*— leaving vast swaths of destruction.

Dickinson's poems have been described as unique in form, unaccountably strange and marvelous, and as having an uncanny psychic urgency and crystalline power. The buried, potentially explosive energetic force of the Nine can be felt in the metaphor of the resting volcano waiting to explode. Feel the bottled up force threatening to break free. It is a poem like this one that allows us to experience poetry's power to engender in us this 'uncanny psychic urgency.'

Note the reference to the *quiet—Earthquake Style*— which very much mirrors the ever calm, quiet, placid shell of the Type Nine, UNTIL the explosion. What had been *too subtle to suspect* now is the *Torrid* symbol of release. Her references to Naples and the North are reminders of Mount Vesuvius erupting in 79 AD and burying the towns of Pompeii and Herculaneum, both near the Southern Italian port of Naples. Little did the *North*, that is the mighty city of Rome, have a clue. We too can be surprised, shocked by the explosion of the Nine, so fooled by the serene countenance.

This forceful poem brings to mind Abraham Lincoln who, as a rule, was a calm, easy-going Kentuckian who was said to have rarely raised his voice. In the Stephen Spielberg 2012 biopic film 'Lincoln,' a pivotal scene is set in which the President's cabinet is arguing with him to drop his efforts to have the 13th Amendment ratified. They feared that the South would step away from the idea of ending the Civil War if the amendment to abolish slavery was forced upon them. Lincoln, who up until then had been carefully and quietly listening to all sides, (a great provenance of the Nine) and considering the heavy burden of the ongoing slaughter of young soldiers as well as the enslavement of human beings (the ability to see both sides) stood suddenly, and with tremendous force, struck the wooden table upon which his hand rested declaring "No!" This is the healthy Nine engaging fully while stepping fully into his or her power. Lincoln took his place and humanity was forever bettered for it.

Dickinson herself wrote hundreds of short poems, many considered strange even today, and she was very fond of the —. Although she freely shared bits of her poetry in her extensive correspondence with family and friends, it was not until her death that her family discovered forty hand-bound volumes of nearly 1800 poems. Under this contained and very quiet exterior lived a fiery woman full of passion and desire. Perhaps she feared that if she let out this passion *Cities* would ooze away— better to keep it all under wraps.

What to Remember When Waking
David Whyte b. 1955

In that first hardly noticed moment in which you wake,
coming back to this life from the other
more secret, moveable and frighteningly honest world
where everything began,
there is a small opening into the new day
which closes the moment you begin your plans.

What you can plan is too small for you to live.
What you can live wholeheartedly will make plans enough
for the vitality hidden in your sleep.

To be human is to become visible,
while carrying what is hidden as a gift to others.
To remember the other world
in this world is to live in your true inheritance.

You are not a troubled guest on this earth,

you are not an accident amidst other accidents,
you were invited from another and greater night
than the one from which you have just emerged.

Now, looking through the slanting light of the
morning window
toward the mountain presence of everything that can
be
what urgency calls you to your one love?
What shape waits in the seed of you
to grow and spread its branches
against a future sky?

Is it waiting in the fertile sea?
In the trees beyond the house?
In the life you can imagine for yourself?
In the open and lovely white page on the writing
desk?

The doorway of transformation for the Nine is the invitation to step into the world, showing up alive and real with the gifts one bears and knowing, truly knowing, that one's presence matters. In these verses we are given a reminder, and as John Keats said, all good poetry is a remembrance. For we are *not a troubled guest on this earth, ... not an accident amidst other accidents.* We have the right to become visible, carrying our gifts to meet life.

The Sonnets of Orpheus 29
Rainer Maria Rilke (1875-1926) translated by
Stephen Mitchell

Silent friend of many distances, feel
how your breath enlarges all of space.
Let your presence ring out like a bell

into the night. What feeds upon your face

grows mighty from the nourishment thus offered.
Move through transformation, out and in.
What is the deepest loss that you have suffered?
If drinking is bitter, change yourself to wine.

In this immeasurable darkness, be the power
that rounds your senses in their magic ring,
the sense of their mysterious encounter.

And if the earthly no longer knows your name,
whisper to the silent earth: I'm flowing.
To the flashing water say: I am.

In the last poem of this exploration of the Nine psyche we return to the genius of Rainer Maria Rilke, once again translated by Stephen Mitchell. It is the last of the sonnets from his 'The Sonnets to Orpheus,' a series of poems in a cycle taking Rilke from his dark and isolated world back into the light of the world. These were written in memory of the death of a young woman, a dear playmate of his daughter Ruth. Rilke's address is to the God Orpheus who, in a famous Greek myth, traveled to the Underworld where he managed to touch the heart of Hades, the God of the Underworld with his exquisite playing of the lyre. So moved, Hades agreed to allow Orpheus' beloved Eurydice to return to life. But Hades had one condition: that Orpheus should not turn back to look upon his love until he reached the light of life. Not trusting that she followed, Orpheus looked back one last time only to see Eurydice dissolve away back into death, losing her forever. He stood between life and death and could not have faith. Orpheus entered life again but brought the sentence of his own death with him, dying a violent death in the few years left to him. Unlike Orpheus Rilke escapes, and like water, is flowing and present and very much alive.

Rilke implores us to *Let your presence ring out like a bell* and he assures us that our impact upon others *What feeds upon your face/grows mighty from the nourishment thus offered.* We make a difference, nourishing those to whom we offer our gifts. Rilke goes on to reassure us, especially the Nine in us which can so easily disappear back into the darkness of anonymity, that we do still exist and have the right to declare *I am.*

Let my hidden weeping arise and blossom.
~ Rainer Maria Rilke
The Tenth Elegy

Four
The individualist

The Four in us is that part that loves depth, intimacy, and beauty. We are in the province of a rich inner life, one pregnant with intuition and creativity, and from this inner world a longing is expressed to know who we *really* are, most especially the unique identity of self. The Four realm is one of penetrating exploration of the deep emotions of life and a craving to enter the dark and explore the exquisite stillness and knowing therein. The Four has a great willingness to look at the dark side of life and thence bring an understanding to the surface, thus profoundly touching and awakening others. Be it Tchaikovsky's haunting *Pathetique,* Keats' exquisite *Ode on Melancholy,* or Frida Kahlo's self-portrait *With a Thorn Necklace*— we the audience are touched deeply and asked to drop down into a world of the tortured heart and with this sense, truly feel a part of life urgent and real.

The great risk lies in the seductive power to believe these dark feelings are all that is life, thus merging with intense emotion and sinking into melancholia and depression. Self-absorption and the feeling that no one can really understand their depth, that life is played in only minor keys, can dominate their persona in a dramatic way. The Four's key to emotional balance and freedom is a movement back to the light that opens with an appreciation for the everyday beauties of life, recognizing that the ordinary, alongside the extraordinary, is also a part of the beauty of life.

Essential Gifts

- Depth, Authenticity and Creativity

Focus of Attention

- Exploring my individual identity

At my Best

- I am unique, intuitive and introspective
- I share the subtleties of my inner life with others

As I lose contact with my Essential Self

- I create strong moods to feel alive
- I withdraw and fantasize about my feelings

When I've lost contact with True Nature

- I can become envious, alienated and see myself as a victim
- I am vulnerable to depression

Doorway to Growth

- Finding the beauty in the ordinary and in myself

Darkness within darkness.
The gateway to all understanding.
~ Lao-Tzu

Pied Beauty
Gerard Manley Hopkins (1844-1889)

Glory be to God for dappled things—
For skies of couple-color as a brinded cow;
For rose-moles all in stipple upon trout that swim;
Fresh-firecoal chestnut-falls; finches' wings;
Landscape plotted and pieced—fold, fallow, and plough;
And all trades, their gear and tackle and trim.

All things counter, original, spare, strange;
Whatever is fickle, freckled (who knows how?)
With swift, slow; sweet, sour; adazzle, dim;
He fathers-forth whose beauty is past change:
Praise him.

The inner life of the withdrawn and original English poet and priest Gerard Manley Hopkins was filled with longings to express the exquisite beauty of his beloved English countryside. His authenticity rattled critics with his first published poem, for here was seemingly topsy-turvy language, let alone the punctuation. So sensitive to being misunderstood, he never offered another poem for publication in his lifetime. We are indebted to his dear friend and future editor Robert Bridges for bringing his poetry to the page nearly thirty years after Hopkin's death.

I've chosen *Pied Beauty* as the first poem to awaken the Essence of the Type Four, for in its originality it is saturated with the imagery of beauty calling us to see the tiniest detail of nature surrounding us. Allow yourself to *see* in your mind's eye a dappled sky overhead filled with clouds at sunset as they are *brinded* (brinded being another word for brindled or dappled, like the brindle coat of a puppy) with the grays, pinks, and salmons of the gloaming, or the exquisite patterns on a wet trout's skin.

When I first arrived in England's far northern Lake district I boarded a bus to take me from the town of Penrith to the village of Keswick where I would live the winter months. It was a late January afternoon and the sun was broken with cloud and shone upon a patchwork of fields, some enclosed with stone walls built to create sheep folds; some fallow, but all pieced like an exquisite quilt fashioned by man of nature's materials. Here was Hopkin's *Landscape plotted and pieced.*

For Hopkins, not only nature's forms elicit admiration, but also man's useful tools: gear, tackle, and trim. He can see the exquisite in the most quotidian of items as well as the grandeur of nature. This is the great gift and Essence of the Four— seeing deeply into the tiniest of things. Hopkins does it with words, Georgia O'Keefe with the painting of a flower, and Leonard Cohen with a musical lyric. We are asked to look ever so closely at the identity of the subject and to feel the wash of glorious beauty envelop and freshen us.

To the Rose upon the Rood of Time
Lines from, W. B. Yeats (1865-1939)

Come near, that no more blinded by man's fate,
I find under the boughs of love and hate,
In all poor foolish things that live a day,
Eternal beauty wandering on her way.

Intense emotion; pondering our individual fate; feeling the palpable presence of beauty in all things created— these qualities occupy the mind and heart of the Type Four part in each of us. In these lines from an early poem Yeats touches the core of the Four temperament naming the potential blinding by over-sensitivity and opening to the beauty in the little things in each lived day. The capacity to see the beauty in the ordinary while retaining the depth of feeling — such a gift of this heart centered personality type.

You Darkness
Rainer Maria Rilke (1875-1926)
translated by David Whyte

You darkness from which I come,
I love you more than all the fires
that fence out the world,
for the fire makes a circle
for everyone
so that no one sees you anymore.

But darkness holds it all;
the shape and the flame,
the animal and myself,
how it holds them,
all powers, all sight—

and it is possible: its great strength
is breaking into my body.

I have faith in the night.

In fact, some Enneagram schools have given the Four personality the name 'The Romantic' pointing to this ease of connection to one's emotion and connection to another. The heart is easily reached, experienced, and often felt in a piercing way, be it with joy or heartbreak.

Songwriter, singer, and actress Amanda McBroom knows this territory well, for she describes this state, reminding us all of our choice to step back, see our emotion and step away from despair and into the light of the sun. Imagery of winter and bitter snows covering the seed perfectly reflect what is so natural to the Four— a heartfelt connection springing from underneath it all.

The story McBroom tells of how the song that launched her career came into being is fascinating. One day in the 1970s she was driving down a Southern California freeway listening to the radio when a song came on: *Magdalena* by Danny O'Keefe sung by Leo Sayer. She loved it and especially the lyric *Your love is like a razor. My heart is just a scar.* But as she drove on she kept thinking about that line and thought, "I don't agree with that sentiment." So she asked herself just what love is if it isn't that. She describes her experience "as if someone had opened a window in the top of my head and words came pouring in." She tells of speeding toward home repeating the words as not to forget them; charging into her house straight to the piano and *The Rose,* in a mere ten minutes, was there. McBroom said she's never written a song so speedily in her entire career and feels grateful that, as she puts it, 'a window opened for me to express my thoughts.' I invite you to open your own inner window, letting in what love truly is.

Sonnet 29
William Shakespeare (1564-1616)

When in disgrace with fortune and men's eyes
I all alone beweep my outcast state,
And trouble deaf heaven with my bootless cries,
And look upon myself and curse my fate,
Wishing me like to one more rich in hope,
Featured like him, like him with friends possessed,
Desiring this man's art, and that man's scope,
With what I most enjoy contented least;
Yet in these thoughts myself almost despising,
Haply I think on thee—and then my state,
Like to the lark at break of day arising
From sullen earth, sings hymns at heaven's gate;
For thy sweet love remembered, such wealth brings
That then I scorn to change my state with kings.

As the Four in us loses contact with our inherent riches of identity, lovability, and worth we may fall into the trap of longing for what we perceive others have that we do not. Longing is a common sentiment when we no longer remember the gifts of our own temperament. Shakespeare, so poignantly, touches this place of longing as his narrator wishes and desires in *thoughts myself almost despising.* The form of Shakespeare's sonnet— sixteen lines, ten syllables in each line with every other line rhyming until the last couplet—creates a flowing structure to carry us along in this state, feeling it intensely through phrases like *beweep my outcast state* and *bootless cries.* As it builds line by line, we are saturated in emotional hunger nearly sinking along with the protagonist into despair until, like light bursting through a bruised dark cloud, we hear the lark sing.

We are lifted into another truth, that of our capacity to love and be loved and experience *such wealth* that we, like our poet, feel a content not to be traded, even for the state of kings.

Sappho (630 BCE- 570BCE)
translated by Aaron Poochigian

That impossible predator,
Eros the Limb-Loosener,
Bitter-sweetly and afresh
Savages my flesh.

Like a gale smiting an oak
On mountainous terrain
Eros, with a stroke,
Shattered my brain.

But a stranger longing to pass on
Seizes me, and I need to see
Lotuses on the dewy banks of Acheron.

Sappho lived in ancient Greece on the Isle of Lesbos as a lyrical poet, most probably the daughter of an aristocratic family. She wrote prolifically and was well read and respected in ancient Greece with Plato naming her 'The Tenth Muse.' Only one entire poem still exists, her *Ode to Aphrodite*, and this poem along with fragments still remaining show us a woman expressing the passions of sexual desire, and the power of this desire devolving into envy and jealousy. I've chosen this fragment of a poem offering a caution to that possessive and at times obsessive power of Eros God of Sexual Attraction, son of Aphrodite Goddess of Love. So powerful is this attraction that our limbs may loosen and our flesh feel savaged. When this Four part in us is taken into Eros' grip, we can feel like *with a stroke* Eros has shattered our brains. We now merge our emotionality with sexual desire and can literally emotionally and mentally self destruct. Vincent Van Gogh comes to mind as he maimed his body lopping off his ear in the throws of desire for his unrequited love.

What is so stunning in these glorious verses is the last three lines in which our narrator describes coming back to herself when *a stranger long to pass on* seized her and she was able to return to tranquility, grounding herself in the image of beauty in the lotus on *the dewy banks of Acheron,* an actual river in Northern Greece that was in Greek Mythology called the river of woe, and in Homer's poems was the River of Hades, the Underworld. We see once again the Four diving into the deep, into the underworld yet stopping, not be swept under in despair, but to appreciate the simple beauty of the flower's bloom. I cannot think of a more helpful image to lift us (like Shakespeare's lark) from the abyss.

Come In

Robert Frost (1875-1963)

As I came to the edge of the woods,
Thrush music—hark!
Now if it was dusk outside,
Inside it was dark.

Too dark in the woods for a bird
By sleight of wing
To better its perch for the night,
Though it still could sing.

The last of the light of the sun

That had died in the west
Still lived for one song more
In a thrush's breast.

Far in the pillared dark
Thrush music went—
Almost like a call to come in
To the dark and lament.

But no, I was out for stars:
I would not come in.
I meant not even if asked,
And I hadn't been.

'A poem begins in delight and ends in wisdom.' So wrote four time Pulitzer Prize winning poet Robert Frost in the foreword to his COLLECTED POEMS. Reciting these stanzas is like swinging on one of Frost's now proverbial birches. Feel the glee as the lines undulate filled with images of light and song and then into the somewhat ominous presence of the dark. Once again sense the seduction for that part of us drawn to the darker expanse of self. As Rilke in this chapter's first poem shows us, here in the dark is great depth and wisdom... but... also the risk of being lost.

Frost was a paradox — a highly practical and energetic man who supported his family as a teacher and then as an apple farmer until his writing (first published in England, not his native America) earned sufficient funds. At the same time he was a melancholic man, prone to deep depression. He had a great creative sensitivity and so often rejoiced in language which he referred to as 'the sound of sense' in the beauty about him. He carried forth the sensibility of the great romantic poet William Wordsworth, England's bard a century before. Frost struggled throughout his life see-sawing between the successful competitive famous writer and the darker aspects of his nature. Here he gives us a doorway to transformation — see the dark but know when it is the right time to *come in.*

Ode on Melancholy

John Keats (1795 - 1821)

I.

No, no, go not to Lethe, neither twist
Wolf's-bane, tight-rooted, for its poisonous wine;
Nor suffer thy pale forehead to be kiss'd
By nightshade, ruby grape of Proserpine;
Make not your rosary of yew-berries,
Nor let the beetle, nor the death-moth be
Your mournful Psyche, nor the downy owl
A partner in your sorrow's mysteries;
For shade to shade will come too drowsily,
And drown the wakeful anguish of the soul.

II.

But when the melancholy fit shall fall
Sudden from heaven like a weeping cloud,
That fosters the droop-headed flowers all,
And hides the green hill in an April shroud;
Then glut thy sorrow on a morning rose,
Or on the rainbow of the salt sand-wave,
Or on the wealth of globed peonies;
Or if thy mistress some rich anger shows,
Emprison her soft hand, and let her rave,
And feed deep, deep upon her peerless eyes.

III.

She dwells with Beauty—Beauty that must die;
And Joy, whose hand is ever at his lips
Bidding adieu; and aching Pleasure nigh,
turning to Poison while the bee-mouth sips:
Ay, in the very temple of delight
Veiled melancholy has her sovran shrine,
Though seen of none save him whose
strenuous tongue
Can burst Joy's grape against his palate fine;
His soul shall taste the sadness of her might,
And be among her cloudy trophies hung.

Ah Keats! I admit to a total devotion to his work filled as it is with gorgeous imagery and joyful celebration of Beauty and Love, all in the full and acknowledged recognition of suffering, loss, and ultimately death to come. This is territory Keats knew well as he nursed his brother, dying of tuberculosis and then, when realizing that he too had contracted the deadly disease, struggled mightily to live, love and continue his work. His are some of the most velvety, sensuous lines ever penned. Here in *Ode on Melancholy* he, like no other poet I know, describes what falling into melancholy is like: *sudden from heaven like a weeping cloud* and just how easily one in this state can be lured into numbing and self annihilation. The River Lethe in Greek Mythology is the river of forgetfulness, of escape from life's woes, while wolf's-bane, deadly nightshade and yew berries are all strong poisons affording likewise an alluring escape. Keats acknowledges he, as we, are *partner in your sorrow's mysteries* tempted to *drown the wakeful anguish of the soul.*

Keats loved life and lived every moment of it until his tragic and painful death from TB. His dear friends gathered to fund his final trip to Italy in hopes that escaping the damp English climate would aid his recovery; but sadly he died in Rome, alone at age twenty-six. It was as if Keats had lived other lives in the realm of the Type Four, grappling with his loss, yearning, and painful sensitivity to beauty to arise like a flame in this current life and blaze brightly with hope, drawing us forward to the preciousness of life. Ah, Keats!

He wishes for the Cloths of Heaven
from *The Wind Among the Trees 1899*
W. B. Yeats (1865-1939)

Had I the heaven's embroidered cloths,
Enwrought with golden and silver light,
The blue and the dim and the dark cloths
Of night and light and the half-light,
I would spread the cloths under your feet:
But I, being poor, have only my dreams;
I have spread my dreams under your feet;
Tread softly because you tread on my dreams.

In this intensely wrought poem we find Yeats a century after Keats giving us the flavor of the Four world and its power to offer, if not actual solid objects of fierce beauty, then of fantasy and dream to bind us together. I love how Yeats acknowledges his vulnerability as he asks his subject to tread softly. Understanding our susceptibility to pain, yet still offering that part of us to another is a pathway to wholeness. I invite you too to *spread your dreams* risking all as you step into the connectivity of all.

The Investigator

[illegible]

Quiet people have the loudest minds.

~ Stephen King

Five
The Investigator

It is the Type Five in us that yearns to explore life, its mysteries and its depth. The desire to understand reality and to seek illumination of the mysteries that shape our existence draw the Five consciousness toward Philosophy and Science and this mining of the psyche is expressed often in Art and Literature. As we see in the Five's neighbor and fellow withdrawn Type Four, there is a depth here likened to the pure darkness of a starry night which Vincent Van Gough captured so brilliantly in his famous painting *Starry Night*. This is the darkness that the great Sufi mystics described as being *alone with the alone*. When the Five loses this sense of knowing, or of even knowing how to go about finding it, then ignorance looms and a kind of existential terror sets in: I don't know why I am here, how I am here, and if there is, as Einstein famously asked, a benevolence in the Universe.

Enneagram scholar and teacher Russ Hudson, himself a Type Five, describes the Five mind as an *inner tinker toy*. Moving from the conceptual and heady inner world out into the practical work of life is the Five's challenge. With their tremendous capacity as great thinkers, they gift us all when they bring their knowledge and depth out into the world and to others.

Essential Gifts

- Curious, Perceptive and Playfully Quirky

Focus of Attention

- Ideas— How things work

At my Best

- I am visionary and pioneering
- I am capable of profound insights

As I lose contact with my Essential Self

- I retreat from participation in the world, drawing into my inner world
- I begin to detach and become secretive

When I've lost contact with True Nature

- I can become isolated, eccentric and cynical

Doorway to Growth

- Reaching out with my gifts to others

> I've been absolutely terrified every moment of my life—and I've never let it keep me from doing a single thing I wanted to do.
> ~ Georgia O'Keefe

Planet
Pablo Neruda (1904-1973), translated by Alastair Reid

Are there stones of water on the moon?
Are there waters of gold?
What color is autumn?
Do the days run into one another
until like a shock of hair
they all unravel? How much falls
—paper, wine, hands, dead bodies—
from the earth on that far place?

Is it there that the drowned live?

Curiosity! Wanting to know, to understand, to know what is where we cannot see, what we can only imagine. Pablo Neruda, lauded Chilean poet-diplomat of the Twentieth Century, gives us discrete and at times disturbing images to flood our own imaginations — the shining image of the rivers of gold on the moon alongside decapitated hands. This is the Essence of the Type Five gift — the capacity to ask, to explore, to vividly see where others may not see. To allow the mind to stretch out beyond the bounds of the everyday, into possibilities. This was Einstein's gift, for who could imagine time as something other than, well, time.

Ah, not to be cut off
Rainer Maria Rilke, translated by Stephen Mitchell

Ah, not to be cut off,
not through the slightest partition
shut out from the law of the stars.

The inner—what is it?
if not intensified sky,
hurled through with birds and deep
with the winds of homecoming.

And here we have the incomparable Rilke asking what this inner world is, so paramount an inquiry for the Type Five in us. Rilke reassures us and asks us to see it with him as a place of safety and security: *intensified sky, hurled through with birds and deep with winds of homecoming.*

To understand— with knowledge leading to understanding — to feel settled, safe and a part of a greater system is the prime focus of the Five consciousness. We too may become part of the *law of the stars*, that is to know our part and realize how we too are necessary, infinitesimal as we may be, to all that exists.

The Three Goals
David Budbill (1940-2016)

The first goal is to see the thing itself
in and for itself, to see it simply and clearly
for what it is.
No symbolism, please.

The second goal is to see each individual thing
as unified, as one, with all the other
ten thousand things.
In this regard, a little wine helps a lot.

The third goal is to grasp the first and the second goals,
to see the universal and the particular,
simultaneously.

Regarding this one, call me when you get it.

David Budbill, American poet and playwright, grew up in the American heartland and attended the famous Union Theologic Seminary (school of Walt Whitman) in New Your City in the 1960s. He took his questions and his wit and moved away from that city of the Beat poets up into the mountains of Vermont where he continued to write poetry, plays and serve as a commentator on National Public Radio's popular show "All Things Considered." I love this poem because it glows with the two greatest gifts which I have benefited from as a reader: The formulating of the Big Questions and the wit of words crafted to delight. We begin with a weighty first goal, almost as if we are in our college Philosophy 101 class, and then the surprise: *No symbolism, please.* I can see Budbill smiling as he wrote it thinking of years of academic strivings to be clever. And then the second goal is helped with a little wine and the last, 'forget abou' it' as my Sicilian Uncle Sonny would have said. Here is a poem inviting deep contemplation while reminding us never to take ourselves too seriously.

Genius
Billy Collins b. 1941

was what they called you in high school
if you tripped on a shoelace in the hall
and all your books went flying.

Or if you walked into an open locker door,
you would be known as Einstein,
who imagined riding a streetcar into infinity.

Later, genius became someone

who could take a sliver of chalk and squire pi
a hundred places out beyond the decimal point,

or a man painting on his back on a scaffold,
or drawing a waterwheel in a margin,
or spinning out a little night music.

But earlier this week on a wooded path,
I thought the swans afloat on the reservoir
were the true geniuses,

the ones who had figured out how to fly,
how to be both beautiful and brutal,
and how to mate for life.

Twenty-four geniuses in all,
for I numbered them as Yeats had done,
deployed upon the calm, crystalline surface—

forty-eight if we count their white reflections,
or an even fifty if you want to throw in me
and the dog running up ahead,

who were at least smart enough to be out
that day—she sniffing the ground,
me with my head up in the bright morning air.

What is genius? How does such appear to another? Billy Collins plays with these questions and tickles us with images like one who could *take a sliver of chalk and squire pi a hundred places out beyond the decimal point.* Picture this nerd of a math student grabbing pi by the arms, "Oh come on now Pi, let's go stroll out into infinity." I would say that Collins shows us here genius at work as he brings us from tired conceptions into fresh perception. He leads us up out of the inner head zone into the bright morning air.

Apple
Brad E. Leithauser b. 1953

Fruit of the tree of knowledge?
Boil it down —
With sugar and a pinch of cinnamon —
You're left with an old-fashioned synonym
For nonsense: applesauce. That's all. For *this* we lost
Our digs in Paradise, yielded the crown
Of Heaven to dig a cold and moldy grave?
Bright Eve learned *nothing — save*
That education isn't worth the cost.

Inventory
Dorothy Parker (1893-1967)

Four be the things I am wiser to know:
Idleness, sorrow, a friend, and a foe.

Four be the things I'd been better without:
Love, curiosity, freckles, and doubt.

Three be the things I shall never attain:
Envy, content, and sufficient champagne.

Three be the things I shall have till I die:
Laughter and hope and a sock in the eye.

These two short poems by masters of biting wit showcase the dark humor so accessible to the Five. They ask us to look from another angle at the commonplace. American poet Brad E. Leithhauser has a degree from Harvard Law and has worked as an international scholar, poet, and teacher, offering his diverse work, from championing the literary culture of Iceland to writing a novel in verse, Darlington's Fall, about an entomologist. In an interview with PBS he described himself as "a poet, interested in structures and what you might call the mathematics of poetry..." One of the great gifts of the Five is to see the entire system, the overview, and then integrate the structure of the parts into the whole and clarify, clarify, and then clarify a wee bit more.— A mathematical formula for poetical genius.

Dorothy Parker is perhaps the best known modern satirist and infamous for her raw cynicism describing the foibles of men and women. Perhaps her genius as a poet, playwright and screen writer (she won the Academy Award in 1937 for the screenplay of 'A Star is Born') emerges from the deep well of her suffering having experienced great loss in her young life, bouts of depressions throughout it, and a suicide attempt. Yet in spite of her often dark view, she was drawn to hope and donated her entire estate upon her death in 1967 to Martin Luther King, Jr. at the height of his civil rights work.

Contraband

Denise Levertov (1923-1997)

The tree of knowledge was the tree of reason.
That's why the taste of it
drove us from Eden. That fruit
was meant to be dried and milled to a fine powder
for use a pinch at a time, a condiment.
God had probably planned to tell us later
about this new pleasure.
                    We stuffed our mouths full of it,
gorged on *but* and *if* and *how* and again

but knowing no better.
It's toxic in large quantities; fumes
swirled in our heads and around us
to form a dense cloud that hardened to steel,
a wall between us and God, Who in Paradise
Not that God is unreasonable—but reason
in such excess was tyranny
and locked us into its own limits, a polished cell
reflecting our own faces. God lives
on the other side of that mirror,
but through the slit where the barrier doesn't
quite touch ground, manages still
to squeeze in—as filtered light,
splinters of fire, a strain of music heard
then lost, then heard again.

To gorge ourselves on knowledge and presume to figure out the mystery that perhaps we were not meant to fully understand but accept seems very much on Denise Levertov's mind here. Levertov spent her life asking, questioning, and exploring the meaning of life, God, and our place in it all. From her declaration at age five that she would be a writer, she never ceased this inquiry. Here she asks what happens when we go too far and risk shutting out even the small sliver where God squeezes in? This is a challenge and risk for the Five in us, that of avariciously gobbling up information, data, knowledge to such an extent that we've lost the space for appreciating mystery, the unexplainable. Like any gift, used in excess it ends by gobbling up itself.

first lesson
Valerie Berry b. 1956

In April we walk—you ask me
the names of things. I say *bay*
laurel, Umbrellularia californica,
also known as pepperwood. But
nothing happens until I crack
the spine of a slender leaf, hold it
to your nose. Suddenly, your face
is full of tree light, saying the
name, over and over.

Valerie Berry is a physician and poet who has dedicated her work to training young clinicians in the art of medicine. She and I worked side by side for many years at Stanford Medical School as we strove to instill in our students humanistic values in their approach to caring for patients. Yes, we taught how to collect key information, name it correctly in medical-ese and create a differential diagnosis, *but* all the while still remembering to open to the essence of that patient. We are so much more than just the sum of our data points. The Five in us does well when we remember to open our bodily senses and be touched in this deep and knowing way and have our faces perhaps *full of tree light.*

Returns
Wislawa Szymborska (1923-2012) trans. by Magnus Kryniski & Robert Maguire

He came home. Said nothing.
Though it was clear something unpleasant had
happened.
He lay down in his suit.

Put his head under the blanket.
Drew up his knees. He's about forty, but not at this moment.
He exists—but only as in his mother's belly
seven layers deep, in protective darkness.
Tomorrow he will give a lecture on homeostasis
in megagalactic cosmonautics.
For now he's curled up, fallen asleep.

The Snail
William Cowper (1731-1800)

To grass, or leaf, or fruit, or wall,
The Snail sticks close, nor fears to fall,
As if he grew there, housed all
    Together.

Within that house secure he hides,
When danger imminent betides
Of storm, or other harm besides,
    Of weather.

Give but his horns the slightest touch,
His self-collecting power is such,
He shrinks into his house, with much
    Displeasure.

Where'er he dwells, he dwells alone,
Except himself has chattels none,
Well satisfied to be his own
    Whole treasure.

This hermit-like his life he leads,
Nor partner of his banquet needs,
And if he meets one, only feeds
    The faster.

Who seeks him must be worse than blind
(He and his house are so combined)
If, finding it, he fails to find
    Its master.

Two poems written as bookends of two centuries, yet expressing the proclivity so familiar to the Five part of us— that tendency to hide away in our shells, self-protect and wall off the world. Wislawa Szymborska, Polish poet and master of bringing the ordinary into the extraordinary gives us a snapshot. Note how she uses periods to stop a line dead. Feel the doors closing. I was particularly amused with our subjects teaching subject: *megagalactic cosmonautics.* He seemingly awakens in the morning but in a way is back asleep in his world of scientific minutia.

William Cowper's snail has its readymade escape— zip back into the safe and dark shell which he carries with him at all times until he may be unexpectedly stepped on and crushed by a child running through the tall grass. What is safe when *he and his house are so combin'd?* Poems, like life, can be taken at many levels.

A Hunting Party

A
Hunting party
Sometimes has a greater chance
Of flushing love and God
Out in the open
Than a warrior
All Alone.

It Felt Love

How
Did the rose
Ever open its heart

And give to the world
All its
Beauty?

It felt the encouragement of light
Against its
Being,

Otherwise,
We all remain

Too

Frightened.

In these two gems by 14th Century Persian poet Hafiz (1315-1390) in the brilliant translations of Daniel Ladinsky we have crystallized wisdom for that part of us that feels fearful to reach out to others, engage and show our faces in a frightening world. We may have ideas, plans, work in progress, intentions all locked away in inaction, doubt, and concern for rejection. Hafiz in his playful way coaxes us out of our defended attitudes and stances. When we are able to come forth, open to life and offer the beauty of our gifts then we too meet heart to heart with humankind.

Tobar Phadraic
David Whyte b. 1955

Turn sideways into the light as they say
the old ones did and disappear
into the originality of it all.

Be impatient with easy explanations
and teach that part of the mind
that wants to know everything
not to begin questions it cannot answer.

Walk the green road above the bay
and the low glinting fields
toward the evening sun, let that Atlantic
gleam be ahead of you and the gray light
of the bay below you, until you catch,
down on your left, the break in the wall,
for just above in the shadows
you'll find it hidden, a curved arm
of rock holding the water close to the mountain,
a just-lit surface smoothing a scattering of coins,
and in the niche above, notes to the dead
and supplications for those who still live.

But for now, you are alone with the transfiguration
and ask no healing for your own
but look down as if looking through time,
as if through a rent veil from the other
side of the question you've refused to ask.

And you remember now, that clear stream
of generosity from which you drank,
how as a child your arms could rise and your palms
turn out to touch the blessing of the world.

Turn sideways into the light — a sentence English/Irish poet David Whyte employs in this poem of choices. In talking about the origin of his poem Whyte tells of the ancient Irish myth of the Tuatha De Danann, a tall magical people who, when facing certain defeat by fierce Milesian invaders, turned sideways into the light and disappeared, not in cowardice but as a choice to take another path; to create a shift in consciousness taking tremendous courage. What does it mean to not seek easy answers, but to teach the eager mind to quiet, open, and expand? For the Five who can so easily live in the heady regions of the mind with the body and heart mere appendages, this poem is a beautiful reminder of what was always there: *that clear stream of generosity from which you drank.* Whyte invites us all, here at the well named Tobar Pahdraic in Old Irish, to stay awake and available for the blessings of the heart.

The Dutiful Types

One
Two
Six

My creed is goodness.
~ Ralph Waldo Emerson

One
The Reformer

The One in us is that part which strives for right action, following our principles with integrity, order, and the sincere desire to right wrongs; to be good and to do good. Service to others is both a responsibility and an ideal. Individuals dominant in this personality type often work in public service as reformers and leaders, be it protecting the environment or campaigning for seat belts in automobiles. Ones tend to be marvelous teachers bringing their innate ability to creatively organize complex material into a framework for learning. They may be drawn to politics where they advocate for change. Think of Ghandi leading his march to the sea, inspiring his people to independence.

This highly responsible part of us, however; is at constant risk of becoming over critical, judgmental, and rigid toward others and indeed, toward ourselves. The Inner Critic voices are clamorous as they scream "No time for rest. Do more— it is your job!" Quieting this inner scolding and finding the balance between having pleasure purely for the sake of joyful fun and continuing one's purposeful labors is an ongoing challenge for the One. As the mind quiets while integrity and purpose soar, the world is gifted with great accomplishment guided by goodness set to a moral compass.

Essential Gifts

- Integrity, Goodness, and Service to a Higher Good

Focus of Attention

- Doing things right with fairness and attention to detail

At my Best

- I am wise, discerning of the right means to the right end
- I am accepting of myself and others

As I lose Contact with my Essential Self

- I can become serious and driven
- I feel the necessity to judge and correct myself and others

When I've lost contact with True Nature

- I can become self-righteous and inflexible
- I am controlling and punitive to myself and others

Doorway to Growth

- Laying down the burden of making life perfect

I tucked my trowser-ends in my boots
and went and had a good time.
~ Walt Whitman

Summary

Pablo Neruda (1904-1973), translated by Alastair Reid

I am pleased at having taken on
so many obligations—in my life
most curious elements accumulated:
gentle ghosts which undid me,
an insistent mineral labor,
an inexplicable wind which ruffled me,
the stab of some wounding kisses, the hard reality
of my brothers,
my insistent need to be always watchful,
my impulse to be myself, only myself
in the weakness of self-pleasuring.
That is why—water on stone—my life was always
singing its way between joy and obligation.

The great Chilean poet and Nobel Prize Winner Pablo Neruda was both poet and ardent political reformer. He has become most famous for his extraordinarily beautiful love poems, yet he was just as passionate about his extensive odes to freedom for the people against the rule of tyrants. This complex man actually wrote his poems in green ink, his personal symbol for desire and hope. Neruda was a lifelong supporter of the ideals of communism, and in 1953 the recipient of the Lenin Peace Prize, a fact surprising many who know him only through his Love Cantos. He was ever concerned with the realization of his great hope for the betterment of living conditions for all peoples.

In *Summary* we are given a succinct, clear, and powerful summary of both the gifts and the struggles of a man working with *an insistent mineral labor* while still being open to *the stab of some wounding kisses.*

Note his choice of words: *obligations, labor, insistent need,* all flavoring the reader's taste of his drive toward his life's work. We can hear clearly his harsh inner critic scolding him for *the weakness of self-pleasuring,* yet he has managed to live his life —*water* (the soft flow of his heartfelt desires) *on stone* (the grounded, solid foundation of his life's purpose). How beautiful is the balance he achieved— a balance we are all invited to achieve, no matter if we are dominant in the Type One temperament or in another, and thusly, like Neruda, live a life *singing its way between joy and obligation.*

From **The Prelude, 1805 Book I**
William Wordsworth (1770-1850)

Far better never to have heard the name
Of zeal and just ambition, than to live
Thus baffled by a mind that every hour
Turns recreant to her tasks, takes heart again,
Then feels immediately some hollow thought
Hang like an interdict upon her hopes.
This is my lot; for either still I find
Some imperfection in the chosen theme,
Or see of absolute accomplishment
Much wanting, so much wanting, in myself,
That I recoil and droop, and seek repose
In listlessness from vain perplexity,
Unprofitably traveling toward the grave,
Like false steward who hath much received
And renders nothing back. - Was it for this
That one, the fairest of all Rivers, loved
To blend his murmurs with my Nurse's song.
And from his alder shades and rocky falls,
And from his fords and shallows, sent a voice
That flow'd along my dreams? For this,

didn't Thou,
O Derwent! traveling over the green Plains
Near my 'sweet Birthplace', did thou,
beauteous Stream,
Make ceaseless music through the night and day
Which with its steady cadence tempering
Our human waywardness, comps'd my thoughts
To more than infant softness, giving me,
Among the fretful dwellings of mankind,
A knowledge, a dim earnest, of the calm
Which Nature breathes among the hills
and groves, ...

William Wordsworth, poet and reformer, struggled throughout his entire life with an ever insistent inner drive to be productive, to reform, and to perfect. In his early twenties he published in collaboration with his great friend and fellow idealist Samuel T. Coleridge "The Lyrical Ballads," a book of poems which revolutionized the language of poetry and became the foundation of future poets from W. B. Yeats to Robert Frost.

Wordsworth was born in the far north of England in the stunning landscape of the Lake District where his childhood home perched upon the banks of the River Derwent. I have stood in his boyhood nursery and listened to the flow of the Derwent as it meandered past his back garden. As I listened to the sounds of running water I thought of how this river soothed a restless soul. For Wordsworth his beloved Lake District with *All the landscape endlessly enriched with waters running, falling and asleep (Prelude Book VIII)* proved his balm for the agitation of mind and spirit so often plaguing him— of his *Zeal and just ambition* as he wrote political pamphlets and traveled to France in the early idealist days of the French Revolution.

You may listen too to the flow of the poem's verses as you read them aloud and feel the gentle lilting movement and the turning of each line (*vertere* Latin for 'to turn') as together they create the calming influence that the poet is recalling here in the first part of his extraordinary autobiographical masterpiece, *The Prelude.* Wordsworth finished the first draft while still a young man but did not allow its publication until after his death; for his entire life he doggedly revised, perfected, and polished even until his final days.

Reading Wordsworth aloud invites in the very sensations — the language of his body and ours, which so help to support us, each in our individual ways, cope with the insistent demands of our inner voices. Wordsworth wasn't the first poet to invoke Nature as *perpetual logic to my soul,* but he was the first to 're-form' standard stilted forms of poetry and literary prose and invoke Nature in simple and direct language as consoler, mentor, and muse. He leaves us forever with his assuring voice to echo in our hearts and minds.

Kind of an Ode to Duty
Ogden Nash (1902-1971)

O Duty,
why hast thou not the visage of a sweetie or a cutie?
Why glitter thy spectacles so ominously?
Why art thou clad so abominously?
Why art thou so different from Venus
and why do thou and I have so few interests
mutually in common
 between us?

Why art thou fifty per cent martyr
And fifty-one per cent Tartar?

Why is it thy unfortunate wont
To try to attract people by calling on them either to leave undone
the deeds they like, or to do the deeds they don't?
Why art thou so like an April post-mortem
Or something that died in the ortumn?
Above all, why dost thou continue to hound me?
Why art thou always albatrossly hanging around me?

Thou so ubiquitous,
And I so iniquitous.

I seem to be the one person in the world thou art perpetually
preaching at who or to who;
Whatever looks like fun, there art thou standing between me and
it, calling yoo-hoo.
O Duty, Duty!
How noble a man should I be hadst thou the visage of a sweetie or
a cutie!
But as it is thou art so much forbiddinger than a Wodehouse hero's
forbiddingest aunt
That in the words of the poet, When Duty whispers low, *Thou*
must, this erstwhile youth replies, I just can't.

Ogden Nash knew how, as former Poet Laureate Robert Hass wrote, to *toss pun, rhyme, and reason about with such brilliance.* Here he lampoons that part of himself fiercely called to 'Duty' — *so different from*

Venus. His line *fifty percent martyr/ And fifty-one percent Tartar* perfectly pokes both fun at and brings to the surface what may be lurking in the ooze, an honest assessment of what we can look like as we fall to the seduction of the dutiful, reforming, finger wagging 'Reformer.'

Nash was an American poet of the Twentieth Century, a restless youth bouncing from St. George's School in Rhode Island to his one year at Harvard and then back again to St. George's where, as an instructor, he said he wrecked his nervous system carving lamb for fourteen-year-olds. Nash became that rarest of birds — the profitable poet who also collaborated on Broadway productions, starred in Comedy reviews, and toured the country speaking and reading his work. Always inventive with language, tempo, sound, and words themselves— for how many times has spellcheck dared to correct the wonderful *ortumn* rhyming with *post-mortem?* Nash brings humor, and like Wordsworth's balm of Nature, Nash offers another means of support — the opportunity to not take ourselves so seriously; to jest, to laugh, to skewer our own high pretensions. In a word, humor.

This is a poem demanding to be read aloud (after practicing a few times words like *abominously* and *forbiddingest) and* allowing along the way the giggling ripples to loosen our grip on whatever it is at the moment driving us on to the role of *martyr* or *Tartar.* His poet's quote *When duty whispers low* is from a famous Type One— Ralph Waldo Emerson whom Nash greatly admired— but; no one has ever claimed that we can't gain insights and gain little suggestions for bits of change while not laughing at the same time. Enjoy!

To Amarantha, that She Would Dishevel Her Hair
Richard Lovelace (1617-1657)

Amarantha sweet and fair,
Ah, braid no more that shining hair!
As my curious hand or eye
Hovering round thee, let it fly!

Let it fly as unconfined
As its calm ravisher, the wind,
Who hath left his darling, th' East,
To wanton o'er that spicy nest.

Every tress must be confest,
But neatly tangled at the best;
Like a cléw of golden thread
Most excellently ravelled.

Do not then wind up that light
In ribbands, and o'ercloud in night,
Like the Sun in's early ray;
But shake your head, and scatter day!

Seventeenth century English poet Richard Lovelace considered himself a 'Cavalier poet' and by that he meant that his task as poet was to offer sage advice on relationships, grief, love, and the pursuit of beauty. In his advice to Amarantha we find Lovelace addressing, in metaphor, that part of us with a tendency to constraint and confinement. How often can we become so worried about form, correctness, and appropriateness that we hold back, wrap up our free intentions as tightly as Amarantha tightly braids her golden hair. Notice images of the release of what is golden: shining hair, golden threads let off their spool, and the ribbons of light in the Sun's rays. So too we may be encouraged to, considering our gifts, to let them fly!

Moderation Is Not A Negation of Intensity, But Helps Avoid Monotony
John Tagliabue (1923-2006)

Will you stop for a while, stop trying to pull yourself
together
for some clear "meaning" — some momentary summary?
no one
can have poetry or dances, prayers or climaxes all day;
the ordinary
blankness of little dramatic consciousness is good for the
health sometimes,
only Dostoevsky can be Dostoevskian at such long
long tumultuous stretches;
look what that intensity did to poor great Van Gogh!;
linger, lunge,
scrounge and be stupid, that doesn't take much centering
of one's forces;
as wise Whitman said "lounge and invite the soul." Get
enough sleep;
and not only because (as Cocteau said) "poetry is the
literature of sleep";
be a dumb bell for a few minutes at least; we don't want
Sunday church bells
ringing constantly.

Will you stop for a while — When I read this line I feel immediately challenged to break out of my habitual 'doing' mode and take stock. Tagliabue has demanded a review of his reader's lifelong habits, and duties. Are we so driven with our important tasks, our self critical demand to 'fulfill our life's purpose' that we forget to *lounge and invite the soul,* opening to a receptivity nearly impossible if we are too much occupied with our 'purpose.' His poem is an invitation to lay back, open to sensation and experience. Who knows what may emerge.

Like my own Sicilian grandparents, Tagliabue was born in Italy and immigrated at age four with his parents to New Jersey, a lushly rural and agricultural state just across the Hudson from the bustling New York City. Tagliabue imbibed both of those influences as a youth, the farmer's fields and fireflies of his home as well as the urban streets and dance clubs of New York's Greenwich Village. At Columbia University he studied alongside the soon to be famous Beat poets Jack Kerouac and Allen Ginsberg who urged him to join their ranks of drop-out poets. Tagliabue declined saying that he instinctively wasn't interested. He followed his own path working his entire life as a teacher and eclectic and lyrical poet, ultimately settling in as a beloved Professor at Bates College in Maine. He was passionate about language, teaching, and dance. This instinctual balance for which he strove — the language of poetry and the movement of dance — defined his great gift for musically singing us into a new perspective.

Today

Mary Oliver b. 1935

Today I'm flying low and I'm
not saying a word.
I'm letting all the voodoos of ambition

sleep.

The world goes on as it must,
the bees in the garden rumbling a little,
the fish leaping, the gnats getting eaten,
And so forth.

But I'm taking the day off.
Quiet as a feather.
I hardly move though really I'm traveling
a terrific distance.

Stillness. One of the doors
into the temple.

Poetry has the power to issue invitations, invitations which we may not even be aware that our deepest nature is craving. This Mary Oliver gem from her brilliant 2012 collection *A Thousand Mornings* is such an invitation. Notice how she echos Wordsworth's *zeal and just ambition* with her *voodoos of ambition.* We can feel the pull, the drive, the justification for putting our ambition above all; yet, here we have another path offered, a path of quiet and stillness where all the efforting drops away leaving us open and receptive to a wisdom quite apart from our own doing.

The Lake Isle of Innisfree
W. B. Yeats

I will arise and go now, and go to Innisfree,
And a small cabin build there, of clay and wattles made:
Nine bean-rows will I have there, a hive for the honey-bee;

And live alone in the bee-loud glade.

And I shall have some peace there, for peace comes dropping
slow,
Dropping from the veils of the morning from where the cricket
sings;
There midnight's all a glimmer, and noon a purple glow,
And evening full of the linnet's wings.

I will arise and go now, for always night and day
I hear lake water lapping with low sounds by the shore;
While I stand on the roadway, or on the pavements grey,
I hear it in the deep heart's core.

What is a doorway through which the busy, doing, striving Type One part of us may step through into serenity? What is the doorway that beckons us to *Arise and go?*

William Butler Yeats, Irish poet, playwright and political figure, so like Wordsworth a century earlier, turns to the simplicity of sensation as he quiets his mind amidst the image of a peaceful abode on the Isle of Innisfree, an uninhabited island within Lough Gill, in County Sligo, Ireland where he spent summers as a child. He described his inspiration for the poem, written when he was twenty-five years old, coming from a "sudden" memory of his childhood while walking down Fleet Street in London. When he heard the tinkle of water from a fountain in a shop-window he remembered the lake water. Up until that time Yeat's poetry had been filled with mythological references and the strict forms of rhetoric. He said this of the poem in an autobiographical piece: "From the sudden remembrance [of the lake] came the poem *Innisfree*, my first lyric with anything in its rhythm of my own music. I had begun to loosen rhythm as an escape from rhetoric...

WH Auden, himself a giant among Twentieth Century poets, praised Yeats as having written some of the most beautiful poetry of modern times. Each time I read, especially aloud, lines like his *There midnight's all a glimmer, and noon a purple glow* I marvel at the ability of a string of words, specifically chosen for sound, color, meter, and flow to transport one into a new way of seeing. As you recite these gently tumbling lines, feel the loosening of your own rhythms of life as *peace comes dropping slow.*

My bounty is as boundless as the sea,
my love as deep, the more I give to
thee,
the more I have, for both are infinite.
~ William Shakespeare
Romeo and Juliet II, ii

Two
The Helper

The Type Two part of us is the capacity to love unconditionally, caring for and nurturing one and other. Loving kindness is a huge value as one heart reaches out to another. With this exquisite attunement to another being, great love pours forth in the world as generosity and the capacity to forgive. Healthy Twos emanate a warmth, sweetness, and quality of genuine caring which touches and supports others. The healthy Two requires no credit and is often the support behind the throne— think of Eleanor Roosevelt to her Franklin.

With the focus so attuned and directed toward the needs of others, the great challenge for this Two part of us lies in forgetting to take notice of our own needs. With such a natural focus on providing for the needs of others, one's own needs can be ignored. To receive help firstly for oneself can feel selfish. When the Essence of Two is blossoming, love and giving are unconditional; however, as image of self takes hold and feels dependent on another's reactions, giving can become conditional — I'll help more, give more so that I'll know by the thank-you and praise that I'm appreciated. I'll convince myself I am truly lovable, no matter the cost.

When this generous part in us can enter into a free flow — no strings attached — of giving *and* receiving, the power of human connection can cascade, healing mankind.

Essential Gifts

- Capacity to love unconditionally with Generosity and Empathy

Focus of Attention

- Relationships and the needs of others

At my Best

- I have a tremendous generosity of spirit
- I am exquisitely aware of my own needs as well as those of others

As I lose Contact with my Essential Self

- I look for ways to please and get closer to others
- I look for responses from others to prove that I am appreciated

When I've lost contact with True Nature

- I can become manipulative, instilling guilt in others

Doorway to Growth

- Enter into the free flow of receiving as well as giving

> Self-love, my liege, is not so vile a sin as self-neglecting.
>
> ~ William Shakespeare
> King Henry V, II, iii

Love Poem
John Frederick Nims (1913-1999)

My clumsiest dear, whose hands shipwreck vases,
At whose quick touch all glasses chip and ring,
Whose palms are bulls in china, burs in linen,
And have no cunning with any soft thing

Except all ill-at-ease fidgeting people:
The refugee uncertain at the door
You make at home; deftly you steady
The drunk clambering on his undulant floor.

Unpredictable dear, the taxi drivers' terror,
Shrinking from far headlights pale as a dime
Yet leaping before apopleptic streetcars—
Misfit in any space. And never on time.

A wrench in clocks and the solar system. Only
With words and people and love you move at ease;
In traffic of wit expertly maneuver
And keep us, all devotion, at your knees.

Forgetting your coffee spreading on our flannel,
Your lipstick grinning on our coat,
So gaily in love's unbreakable heaven
Our souls on glory of spilt bourbon float.

Be with me, darling, early and late. Smash glasses—
I will study wry music for your sake.
For should your hands drop white and empty
All the toys of the world would break.

When I came across this poem in “How Does a Poem Mean?” by John Ciardi I was stunned to feel so keenly and identify with so deeply the Essence of the Type Two. John Frederick Nims was an American poet of great stature, equally as famous as translator of the poetry of Sappho and Michelangelo as he was as beloved Professor and inspiration to young writers. He must have known intimately the tremendous impact of the warmth, generosity, and unconditional love of a Type Two who was perhaps his wife or one of his daughters. Note that Nims is not calling attention to physical signs of beauty, so often the trope of love poems, but to the core of the interiority of his *darling.* It is how she is— her being: *The refugee uncertain at the door/You make at home:deftly you steady/The drunk clambering on his undulant floor.*

In the opening line *my clumsiest dear* we hear Nims set the foundational warmth of the piece (so like the Type Two herself) and we can chuckle at his dear’s daily little domestic disasters while feeling her so essentially a part of *love’s unbreakable heaven.* This is the heaven that is safe, accepting, and loving for all, the heaven exemplifying the knowing that we are cared for and nurtured without having had to earn such love.

Nims ends with an image of the potential loss of this holding sweetness in his life: *For should your hands drop white and empty/All the toys of the world would break.* I would suggest that the image of the toys of the world breaking is the falling away of the clean, simple, capacity to bring comfort and joy to another, a falling away of little pieces of soothing play. When this is lost, its absence is devastating not only to the individual closest to this person, but likewise to the entirety of human connection as it is felt in the greater expanse of universal energy. As the latest particle physics shows us, we are all connected atom to atom across the vastness of time and space. The beautiful quality of the Type Two is in the glue of that connection.

She Walks in Beauty
Lord Byron (George Gordon) (1788-1824)

She walks in beauty, like the night
Of cloudless climes and starry skies;
And all that's best of dark and bright
Meet in her aspect and her eyes;
Thus mellowed to that tender light
Which heaven to gaudy day denies.

One shade the more, one ray the less,
Had half impaired the nameless grace
Which waves in every raven tress,
Or softly lightens o'er her face;
Where thoughts serenely sweet express,
How pure, how dear their dwelling-place.

And on that cheek, and o'er that brow,
So soft, so calm, yet eloquent,
The smiles that win, the tints that glow,
But tell of days in goodness spent,
A mind at peace with all below,
A heart whose love is innocent!

She Walks in Beauty must surely be the most famous poem the flamboyant, multi-faceted and prolific Lord Byron ever wrote. Byron was a man of paradox — equally absorbed in the freedom of his passionate bisexual affairs as he was about his fervent reading of the Bible and the Calvinistic sense of original sin. He said that he wrote this poem after seeing his cousin at a party wearing a mourning dress with spangles on it. He is seeing the woman as well as the dressing— the inner and the outer raiments of beauty.

I've chosen this poem specifically to ask you reader to look afresh at something familiar. What does it mean to walk in beauty? The Navajo Indians have that very phrase at the core of their spiritual connection to the Great Spirit, their creator and deity. To *walk in beauty* is to be in harmony with one's place on the earth and one's place in the greater universe of love and connection. There is an uncomplicated purity about the image, the image of pure unconditional love and innocence. Byron strikes the chord in his last lines as he describes this quality, the Essence of the point Two, and its impact upon himself.

She Walks in Beauty is known in general as a romantic love poem written by one of the most famous of Romantic Poets of all time, yet it seems to me to speak to an overall presence of innocent, peaceful love imbued with goodness. This is no ode to a specific female, but an ode to the sweetness *so soft, so calm, yet eloquent/the smiles that win, the tints that glow* of the part so integral to the point Two; yet, most assuredly, a glow that exists in each of us as well.

The Clod and the Pebble
William Blake (1757-1827)

"Love seeketh not itself to please,
Nor for itself hath any care,
But for another gives its ease,
And builds a Heaven in Hell's despair."

So sung a little Clod of Clay
Trodden with the cattle's feet,

But a Pebble of the brook
Warbled out these metres meet:

"Love seeketh only self to please,
To bind another to its delight,
Joys in another's loss of ease,
And builds a Hell in Heaven's despite."

What happens when we misuse our gift of love, when we wield our generosity as a device to elicit something from another? And why would one do this? For that insecure part of us: If I'm appreciated then that translates into I'm ok, I'm lovable. The entire action becomes the act of giving conditionally, giving to get back what I don't believe I already have — inherent lovability. The result is that the Essence quality of no-strings love is turned upside down into a kind of manipulation. Blake pulled no punches. Instead of building a Heaven in Hell's despair quite the opposite is achieved as building a Hell in Heaven's despite the 'good intentions.'

William Blake was a remarkable man in a remarkable time of revolutionary spirit. During his lifetime he was most known as an artist and engraver and sadly died penniless in the arms of his beloved wife of forty-five years while making the illustrations for Dante's *Inferno* in which the Devil is frozen in ice at the very apex of the cone of the narrowing inferno. As Dante descends into this constricted frozen floor of Hell he must physically somersault over on himself in order to ascend back up toward Heaven. I've always wondered if Blake, who so naturally saw in visions and images, had this scene in mind as he takes the sacred 'Love' and turns it on its head.

Blake spent his life rallying against oppression based on race, gender, or religious preference. He was a stanch opponent of slavery and a great supporter of women's rights and became associated with the 'free love' movement of the day. It feels particularly poignant that he here gives us this little dialogue between an easily crushable clod of clay being trampled upon and a solid pebble standing firmly in the bed of the stream. Love given to get is easily crushed, trampled upon by the response, or lack thereof. It is fragile and easily destroyed. Love given not to get is firm and durable as the image of the little pebble amidst the flowing beck. For the point Two in each of us the question and caution beams out brightly— are we manipulating with our generosity, with our love or are we giving it innocently, purely, and freely. 'Free love' is precisely that, free for the giving.

Over Wine
Wislawa Szymborska (1923-2012)

He glanced, gave me extra charm
and I took it as my own.
Happily I gulped a star.

I let myself be invented,
modeled on my own reflection
in his eyes. I dance, dance, dance
in the stir of sudden wings.

The chair's a chair, the wine is wine,
in a wineglass that's the wineglass
standing there by standing there.
Only I'm imaginary,
make-believe beyond belief;
so fictitious that it hurts.

And I tell him tales about

ants that die of love beneath
a dandelion's constellation.
I swear a white rose will sing
if you sprinkle it with wine.

I laugh and I tilt my head
cautiously, as if to check
whether the invention works.
I dance, dance inside my stunned
skin, in his arms that create me.

Eve from the rib, Venus from foam,
Minerva from Jupiter's head—
all three were more real than me.

When he isn't looking at me,
I try to catch my reflection
on the wall. And see the nail
where a picture used to be.

What does it mean to look to another for your self-worth? How does it feel to erase yourself and become only the reflection of what another shows you? And then when the picture, that image of yourself, is gone you *see the nail / where a picture used to be.* The Polish poet and winner of the 1996 Nobel Prize Wislawa Szymborska was renowned for her knack of being able to take a small domestic scene and imbue it with a universal life meaning. Here Szymborksa touches that sensitive nerve living within the Type Two psyche, that of an exquisite sensitivity to the image we create and feel we need to uphold in order to be desired and loved. The most relational of all the personality types, the Two in us is at risk of forgetting our own magnitude for lovability by placing the validity and quantity of it into the hands of another.

As the poet narrator tells us *I let myself be invented/modeled by my own reflection/in his eyes.* Notice that her perceived reality is that which is only a reflection, not actually herself. What she is seen as becomes who she sees herself as. So when that attention is turned away despite one's actions to hold it, *I laugh and tilt my head*, losing her own identity as she feels erased.

I recall a time amidst the turbulent breakup of a long term relationship when I tried everything I knew to elicit the love and caring I so wished for; I so longed to be cherished. A mentor of mine reminded me of this line, a 'mantra of the type Two' as he described it which I've never forgotten: "Throw me some scraps, just don't throw me away." When the end came with angry rejection and he walked out, I dissolved. I recall feeling like a clay pot, smashed and crumbled to red dust on a desert floor. All sense of who I was, what I was, the beauty that was me — gone. This is the territory of the Two who enters into the dark abyss, but in actuality is then an inchoate fine matter from which to reconstitute the *worse stung heart* as poet Mary Oliver described it. Rejection, the realization that I am erased becomes the genesis for a new birth in true self, that is, if core Essence can be remembered and touched. The pain is real and necessary.

This painful poem I've included in the hopes that it can remind us of *that* part in all of us, but most especially those men and women who put their hearts into another's hands for authenticating. The heart needs it not, for at our core we are all of value, of worth, and are able to be truly loved.

The Sun Never Says
Hafiz (1320-1389)
translated by Daniel Ladinsky

Even
After
All this time.
The sun never says to the earth,

"You owe
Me."

Look
What happens
With a love like that,
It lights the Whole Sky.

Here the Twelfth Century Persian poet and Sufi Master offers a little gem of a poem pointing to what is often most easily forgotten when our sense of self orbits about the notion that we can only be worthy of love if we are getting recognition in return, or a pay back of sorts. I'm reminded of the reaction I once (I'm most ashamed to admit now) felt when I didn't receive a thank-you note for a gift I'd sent to my niece. "Well, that's it for her," I said. "No more gifts if she isn't going to be grateful." I see how it was really all about me and what I needed to feel like the lovable Auntie, and not about the simple joy of sending this lovely young girl a special gift. Notice how I literally stopped the loving in its tracts.

Once the Two in us releases the strings attached to giving and simply loves cleanly, unconditionally, then all is possible. As Hafiz says: *With a love like that,/It lights [the sun] the Whole Sky.*

Woken In the Night by Contents Under Pressure
Patti Tronolone b. 1952

I long to let my spirit fly free
To set out high and wide beyond the proper precincts
To go before me and trail long behind
The baffling and often confusing margins of my body.

I would be a sail of a great ship
Riding the ancient waters like a wild horse
Who confesses the unbroken borders of the Eternal
In which there can be discovered no parting seam.

I long to let my spirit fly free
If once to know its splendor unfurled
To spot the source of its sovereignty unrefined
To glimpse its fluid and billowing glide,
Radiant and alive in the sky's wind.

There would be no shame about its size in this world
But only an instinctual loft and reach
And a lawless desire to stretch and bloom
A God-flower as might be growing in this soul's
breath.

I long to let my spirit fly free
To know one day what and who I am
Beneath and beyond this personal skin
The fearless life of an unmetered and unbeaten
presence on earth
Finally and unwittingly triumphantly free.

The Type Two temperament is greatly concerned with Image, that is, how I appear to others in my physical presentation, my speech, my actions. Trusting what is real *beyond this personal skin* is the great challenge. Patti Tronolone is a master Reiki healer and poet who sees beneath the skin into the energies of the men and women with whom she works. She reminds us here that we have the potential to ride *the ancient waters like a wild horse* as we live authentically without shame, letting our own spirits fly free. I believe the invitation is to *stretch and bloom* beyond the false image we may habitually see ourselves as.

Lending Out books
Hal Sirowitz b. 1949

You're always giving, my therapist said.
You have to learn how to take. Whenever
you meet a woman, the first thing you do
is lend her your books. You think she'll
have to see you again in order to return them.
But what happens is, she doesn't have the time
to read them, & she's afraid if she sees you again
you'll expect her to talk about them, & will
want to lend her even more. So she
cancels the date. You end up losing
a lot of books. You should borrow hers.

The great and fundamental gateway for the Two personality's opportunity for real change is the practice of not only giving, but receiving. Hal Sirowitz is a retired New York City special ed school teacher whose first collection of poems "My Mother Said" and his soon to follow "My Therapist Said" touched a deep chord in readers. His books quickly sold out, an uncommon occurrence in the modern poetry scene to be sure. Sirowitz became known in many circles as the 'people's poet,' his work being translated into thirteen languages. Why? I think because he so precisely identifies and, with a light and humorous hand, points to the habits of behavior which so reliably trip us up.

I laughed out loud when I first read *Lending Out Books* as I remembered loaning out a beloved first edition copy of *Smoky*, the classic western novel by Owen Wistler. When I eventually asked my friend, an elderly gentleman, if he might return it he replied that he'd loaned it to a fellow he met at the library. My dear friend died that autumn and along with it the chance to recover my book. My motto back then was something like 'Give first and think about the value of what you gave later.' I no longer loan out precious items unless I consider them a gift. The receiving comes in when I allow myself *not* to give, holding the gift to myself. Each time I do this I'll admit it feels uncomfortable, sort of ungracious and selfish, but it is getting easier and feels clean, uncluttered, and downright refreshing.

Ralph Waldo Emerson said this of successful poetry in his essay On Poetry: It astonishes and fires us with new endeavors. My endeavor is in taking Sirowitz's advice seriously — I'll ask for something for myself before I give— astonishing for the Type Two and a reminder for those who love us.

The whole course of things goes to teach us faith. We need only obey. There is guidance for each of us, and by lowly listening we shall hear the right word.

~ Ralph Waldo Emerson, Spiritual Laws

Six
The Loyalist

The Type Six part of us is the capacity to know how to participate in this risky world and how to deal with its challenges. Amidst this process of searching for guidance, alertness and a skeptical scanning run continuously, always looking for what is trustworthy and dependable. When at our best, we are loyal to our cause and lend a stability to our environment. We take our duty seriously to have the back of those around us. Think of Samwise Gamgee, Frodo's great friend in JRR Tolkien's *Lord of the Rings*, who sticks with Frodo through the very fires of Mordor, all the way until the task is completed. This is the beautiful quality of the healthy Type Six.

Like any gift, when overdone these very same assets become liabilities, and so alertness may become suspicion and vigilance paranoia. Tremendous anxiety takes grip and the mind spins— *worry, fret, worry*— not knowing who or what to trust. When the anxiety reaches an intolerable level we can abruptly react, popping off like a steam vent. The formerly easygoing colleague becomes the spinning cyclone whose emotional intensity can cut a swath through the workplace. "Where did *that* come from?"

As we quiet the mind and open to an inner knowing, we begin to trust and recognize all the support we actually have in our lives. Opening to Faith, a form of understanding through which force enters into us, we can function in the world with courage and purpose in peace and security. The healthy Six engenders safety for us all.

Essential Gifts

- Trustworthy, Committed and Aware

Focus of Attention

- How can I be safe and secure and know what can go wrong?

At my Best

- I am self-reliant, secure, and can act decisively and courageously

As I lose Contact with my Essential Self

- I become agitated and reactive as I feel helpless
- I can see negative catastrophes everywhere

When I've lost contact with True Nature

- I can become panicky, suspicious and lash out at others

Doorway to Growth

- Letting go of looking for every possible problem

In returning and rest you shall be saved;
In quietness and in trust shall be your strength.

~Isiah 30:15

No Rack can torture me
Emily Dickinson (1830-1886)

384

No Rack can torture me—
My Soul—at Liberty—
Behind this mortal Bone
There knits a bolder One—

You cannot prick with saw—
Nor pierce with Scimitar—
Two Bodies—therefore be—
Bind One—The Other fly—

The Eagle of his Nest
No easier divest—
And gain the Sky
Than mayest Thou—

Except Thyself may be
Thine Enemy—
Captivity is Consciousness—
So's Liberty.

I know of no other poem that so perfectly captures the paradox of the Six temperament: A solid inner knowing which *you cannot prick with saw— Nor pierce with Scimitar—* and the torture of the nagging doubt of the soul which is in captivity of one's own mind, while at the same time that very mind can grant liberty, a freedom from the self torture. Emily Dickinson was an entirely original poet who with razor sharp word selection pierced an idea, rattling our usual perceptions about core human dilemmas.

Within our single being of *mortal Bone* we have both the capacity for a clear and sure mind as well as the apparatus to twist that same mind into knots which act as our own enemy.

Everything Is Going To Be All Right
Derek Mahon b. 1941

How should I not be glad to contemplate
the clouds clearing beyond the dormer window
and a high tide reflected on the ceiling?
There will be dying, there will be dying,
but there is no need to go into that.
The poems flow from the hand unbidden
and the hidden source is the watchful heart;
the sun rises in spite of everything
and the far cites are beautiful and bright.
I lie here in a riot of sunlight
watching the day break and the clouds flying.
Everything is going to be all right.

Again, as in Dickinson's short poem, we see the paradox of acknowledgment that *There will be dying, there will by dying,* (Mahon grew up in Belfast, Northern Ireland at the time of tremendous upheaval, conflict, and change) while we gaze with the poet open the beauty of clouds and reflected tides. Mahon uses the word *should* early on as to me a kind of doubting of his own abilities, a skeptical question to himself. He is letting us into the world of the Type Six consciousness. And what supports this? ... *the watchful heart.* When the busy dutiful mind is much occupied with figuring it all out, it is the open heart that enters to give much needed calm and support. Somehow holding the reality of dying simultaneously with the exquisite beauty at hand, Mahon implies and thusly reassures not only himself but his reader that there exists a timeless weave of the fabric of our existence here on this earth and that *Everything is going to be all right.*

Maps
Holly Ordway

Antique maps, with curlicues of ink
As borders, framing what we know, like pages
From a book of travelers' tales: look,
Here in the margin, tiny ships at sail.
No-nonsense maps from family trips: each state
Traced out in color-coded numbered highways,
A web of roads with labeled city-dots
Punctuating the route and its slow stories.
Now GPS puts me right at the centre,
A Ptolemaic shift in my perspective.
Pinned where I am, right now, somewhere, I turn
And turn to orient myself. I have
Directions calculated, maps at hand:
Hopelessly lost till I look up at last.

Looking for guidance and direction is such a powerful theme for the Type Six individual. I love how this poem, written in a sonnet form: the first eight lines and then a transition, a break, a paradigm shift to the last six lines. Ordway gives us first images of maps with which we are all so familiar; cozy images of where we can look externally and find our way. And then the break — boom! — the world of GPS where we are tracked and located as a pinpoint. The Ptolemaic shift, from the earth/man centered universe to the earth as the satellite orbiting the sun. Here is the paradox of the poem to shock us— man no longer to find guidance by looking at externals of man, but by seeing himself in the larger picture of creation, going deeper for the inner guidance that is transmitted not from external cues, what others say, rewards we've earned; but from a far deeper source. Again think of the paradox facing the dutiful, loyal Type Six person: do I get hooked by life's events, opinions, and values or do I go deeper for foundational support and guidance. Holly Ordway is a remarkable American poet and academic who turned herself upside down by moving from secular academia to Christian themes of imagination and the heart. She encourages us to *look up at last.*

The Panic Bird
Robert Phillips b. 1938

just flew inside my chest. Some
days it lights inside my brain,
but today it's in my bonehouse,
rattling ribs like a birdcage.

If I saw it coming, I'd fend it
off with machete or baseball bat.
Or grab its scrawny hackled neck,
wring it like a wet dishrag.

But it approaches from behind
Too late I sense it at my back—
carrion, garbage, excrement.
Once inside me it preens, roosts,

vulture on a public utility pole.
Next it flaps, it cries, it glares,
it rages, it struts, it thrusts
its clacking beak into my liver,

my guts, my heart, rips off strips.
I fill with black blood, black bile.
This may last minutes or days.
Then it lifts sickle-shaped wings,

rises, is gone, leaving a residue—
foul breath, droppings, molted midnight
feather. And life continues.
And then I'm prey to panic again.

Over my medical career I've worked with many patients who suffered from panic disorder. I think that they would all agree with this gut wrenching description. I've chosen this vivid poem to illustrate the grip anxiety can have on the Type Six, perhaps more so than any other type. Anxiety can cripple and leave the brain sizzling and frozen in the experience of a panic attack. For those of us who have never suffered one of these thefts of the calm mind, listen and bring compassion. The Type Six will know.

Crooked Deals
Hafiz (1315-1390) translated by Daniel Ladinsky

There is
A madman inside of you
Who is always running for office —
Why vote him in,
For he never keeps the accounts straight.
He gets all kinds of crooked deals
Happening all over town
That will just give you a big headache
And glue to your kisser
A gigantic
Confused
Frown.

If the Shoe Doesn't Fit
Naomi Shihab Nye, b. 1952

you take it off
of course you take it off
it doesn't worry you
it isn't your shoe

Find a Better Job
Hafiz
trans. by Daniel Ladinsky

Now
That
All your worry
Has proved such an
Unlucrative
Business,
Why
Not
Find a better
Job.

These three little poems speak to the anxiety and worry and what might be called a *pre*-traumatic stress syndrome from which the Six temperament is so often afflicted. How to stay safe, how to keep those you love safe, and how to know from whom to get the best advice to stay safe are all prime concerns in this domain of consciousness. Hafiz and Nye, from across cultures and ages, bring their wit and humor to lighten the scene, pointing out—well, the obvious! Those with this temperament are known for their own quirky wit and humor so I'm thinking that a dose of the same just might do the trick.

Maybe Not
Danna Faulds

Begin somewhere.
Take one deep breath
and dive.
Plunge into the core
of your most
persistent fear,
or your greatest joy.
Grow comfortable
with the act of
exploration,
Well, maybe
not comfortable,
but confident of
your ability to be
sure footed
on slick rocks,
steady while the
winds gust.
Well, maybe not
entirely confident,
but willing to set out
despite persistent
doubts, breathing
your way into
whatever you are facing.
Well, maybe not even
all that willing,
but you take it
anyway, that first step
into the unknown.
Courage is starting
where there is

no secure outcome,
no sure result.
The secret is you can
begin again at any time.
Take one deep breath,
and dive.

Danna Faulds is a yoga teacher, musician, and as we see here a wonderful poet. What caught my eye so delightfully in her streaming lines is the stuttering quality *Well, maybe not* that punctuates the cascade of the dive she invites us to take into the world of seeking courage and knowing how to put that first step into the unknown. The Six temperament in all of us knows these interruptions of niggling doubt well. Just when resolve seems to have arrived — fresh, strong and alive — in shoehorns the self-doubt. Well...... maybe this or maybe that or maybe even this or that. Faulds shares her secret: in each and every intake of air, we do indeed have the chance to begin again and take that *one deep breath, and dive.*

Ars Poetica
Leslie McGrath

To have
even a
lotto chance

of getting
somewhere
wishing yourself

you don't quite know
but feel

To cling
to the periphery
through the constant

gyroscopic
re-drawing of its
provinces

To make
What Makers make

you must set aside
certainty

Leave it
a lumpy backpack
by the ticket window
at the station

Let the gentleman
in pleated khakis
pressed for time

claim it

The certainty
not the poem.

Leslie McGrath said about her poem on the Academy of American Poets website **poets.org** where I came across this slim treasure of a poem "I wrote 'Ars Poetica' with my students in mind, nudging them away from pursuing a poem as a goal, encouraging them to be more comfortable with uncertainty." Bingo! Here is the core theme for the Type Six. How do we become more comfortable (if indeed we are ever comfortable at all) with uncertainty? What can we trust? What can we *know* to be the correct route to the goal? How can we proceed? Danna Faulds asks us to take a breath and dive, Leslie McGrath asks us to set our uncertainty aside and to *Leave it/a lumpy backpack/by the ticket window/at the station.* The images both poets use give us a visual to hang on to, to grasp and ground when the swirling short circuit of anxiety around a decision commences to buzz. Buzz, buzz, buzz.... hear that sibilant zzzzzz so like the sounds of agitated horse flies about your sweaty head as you hike and come to a fork in the trail. We all have a moment to stop and grasp it, observe what we are experiencing (while we send our inner judge on vacation to the Jersey shore) and claim our right *not* to let the energy sapping negativity of the buzzing doubt drain us, frighten us, and in essence muddle our brain. We have the right to claim our own uncertainty and rest in a trust that, as all things do eventually happen no matter how hard we try or not; a result will unfold.

Matthew 14:22
John S. Clarfield

Step out on faith
like Peter
into yielding waters

knowing the sweet sustain
of doubt suspended

lies in the boat forgotten
in the hand extended.

"Come..."

My Jesus calls.
  My heart rejoices.

While teaching a class on the Poetry of Gerard Manley Hopkins at my church I met John Clarfield, a retired Berkeley librarian. His sweet poem captured for me the essence of the Gospel story of Jesus summoning his disciple Peter to step out of the boat and walk to him across the water. It was the hand offered as assurance that Jesus extended, as we have in our own individual spiritual teachings extended hands offering to help us. Our decision is whether or not to trust that help. Peter did indeed begin to walk upon the water, but then realizing (we can almost hear his 'common sense' screaming at him "YOU can't walk on water, you fool!) he falls into the waves and it is Jesus who plucks him out. Clarfield invites us too to *know the sweet sustain/ of doubt suspended.*

Reaper
Billy Collins b. 1941

As I drove north along a country road
on a bright spring morning
I caught the look of a man on the roadside
who was carrying an enormous scythe on his
shoulder.

He was not wearing a long black cloak
with a hood to conceal his skull—
rather a torn white tee-shirt
and a pair of loose khaki trousers.

But still, as I flew past him,
he turned and met my glance
as if I had an appointment in Samarra,

not just the usual lunch a the Raccoon Lodge.

There was no sign I could give him
in that instant—no casual wave,
or thumbs-up, no two-fingered V
that would ease the jolt of fear

whose voltage ran from my ankles
to my scalp—just the glimpse,
the split-second lock of the pupils
like catching the eye of a stranger on a passing train.

And there was nothing to do
but keep driving, turn off the radio,
and notice how white the houses were,
how red the barns, and green the sloping fields.

We are all destined to 'shuffle off this mortal coil' as Shakespeare's Hamlet tells us in his grand contemplative soliloque on death. Here in everyday and comical images *lunch at the Raccoon Lodge* the extraordinary poet of our modern day Billy Collins brings us to an encounter with a *Rebel Without a Cause* James Dean version of the Grim Reaper walking along a country road. Notice how Collins rattles our perception placing the location *Samarra* (metaphor for the place of death) directly above *Raccoon Lodge* in the dead center of the poem. We may fool ourselves into ignoring our mortal fate, much occupied with mundane chores, but there it is, here a tee-shirted reminder of the mere flash of time we have on this earth. The shock our country driver experiences whose *voltage ran from my ankles/to my scalp...* is it not what we can all make use of in order to summon us to *Awaken!* and look about us and notice the tiniest miracle of our earth. No matter what is around that country corner, we are here *now*, and in this *Now* there is power and beauty and love.

The Assertive Types

Seven Eight Three

Exuberance is Beauty
~ William Blake

Seven
The Enthusiast

Often referred to as the spark plugs of the Enneagram, the Type Seven in us is the sizzling outward energy of exuberance, joy, and unbound freedom. Everything about the Seven domain is geared toward the experiences of possibility and freedom as they joyfully celebrate life. Their great gift is the positivity and hope they bring to others.

Vivacity is a key quality of the Seven. Think of Benjamin Franklin and all of his glorious accomplishments from the investigation of electricity (how fitting!) to his diplomacy skills. Or to the author of America's Declaration of Independence Thomas Jefferson who listed the right to happiness and freedom as core American values. However; the dark side of the Seven temperament lies in a decided avoidance of whatever feels quotidian, routine, and ordinary and certainly anything that is boring — the anathema of the Seven! Sevens are great at imagining and anticipating but are often challenged with the follow-through. When painful experiences threaten the experience of joy, the Seven in us is at risk of escaping away into pleasurable distraction. Yet, when the Seven opens to all of human experience, the beauty and the terror, wonderful things grace us all, for we can see them perhaps as I have, a Hospice worker sitting joyfully in awe of every minute of life helping a patient along the last steps of life's journey.

Essential Gifts

- Exuberance with a joyful, imaginative energy

Focus of Attention

- What's next

At my Best

- I bring high energy to all that I accomplish
- I am joyful and grateful in each and every moment

As I lose contact with my Essential Self

- I become scattered and restless
- I fail to follow through on my ideas and plans

When I've lost contact with True Nature

- I can become dangerously impulsive
- My activities spin out of control

Doorway to Growth

- The realization that I have enough

> From this hour, freedom! From this hour I ordain myself loos'd of limits and imaginary lines.
>
> ~ Walt Whitman, The Open Road

Excerpts from Song of the Open Road
Walt Whitman (1819-1892)

From this hour, freedom!
From this hour I ordain myself loos'd of limits and imaginary lines,
Going where I list, my own master, total and absolute,
Listening to others, and considering well what they say,
Pausing, searching, receiving, contemplating,
Gently, but with undeniable will, divesting myself of the holds that would hold me.

I inhale great draughts of space;
The east and the west are mine, and the north and the south are mine.

I am larger, better than I thought;
I did not know I held so much goodness.

I will recruit for myself and you as I go;
I will scatter myself among men and women as I go;
I will toss the new gladness and roughness among them;
Whoever denies me, it shall not trouble me;
Whoever accepts me, he or she shall be blessed, and shall bless me.

Exemplifying the robust optimism of the Type Seven temperament, Walt Whitman was truly an American original. Freedom! singing through his work as I recall some of his poem titles: *I Sing the Body Electric; I Hear America Singing: Are you the New Person Drawn Toward Me?* He broke free from conventions of his day, creating his own unique 'long line' of poetry unfettering himself from usual schemes of rhyme and rhythm. Read him aloud and you'll find yourself sailing along as if on skates on an icy, smooth and mirrored pond. No poet captures the Essence of the Seven as he does, literally singing out his credo of freedom, curiosity, receptivity, and goodness. His energy pulses forward, never lagging yet paying homage to the value of contemplation. And to think that his formal education ended at age eleven!

Mozart, for Example
Mary Oliver b. 1935

All the quick notes
Mozart didn't have time to use
before he entered the cloud-boat

are falling now from the beaks
of the finches
that have gathered from the joyous summer

into the hard winter
and, like Mozart, they speak of nothing
but light and delight,

though it is true, the heavy blades of the world
are still pounding underneath.
And this is what you can do too, maybe,

if you live simply and with a lyrical heart
in the cumbered neighborhoods or even,
as Mozart sometimes managed to, in a palace,

offering tune after tune after tune,
making some hard-hearted prince
prudent and kind, just by being happy.

Here Mary Oliver, modern grand dame and literary descendant of luminaries Wordsworth, LeMare, and Frost, pays homage to a glorious Type Seven, Wolfgang Amadeus Mozart whose music can still draw a smile from the direst of downcasts. She poses that *if you live simply and with a lyrical heart* you too could impact others about you *by just being happy,* the great gift of the expressive and exuberant Type Seven. I recall a Hospice nurse with whom I had the privilege of working during my years as a family doctor. He had a way about him: totally present to his patient walking beside him or her in the last steps of the journey while radiating a joyful presence helping that patient to a peaceful and fear-free transition. Simply put, he emanated joy. It is no small gift in this life so laden with *the heavy blades of the world.*

One Crowded Hour
Sir Walter Scott (1771-1832)

Sound, sound the clarion, fill the fife!
    To all the sensual world proclaim,
One crowded hour of glorious life
    Is worth an age without a name.

Haiku
Basho (1644-1694)

A bee
staggers out
of the peony.

I love both of these kernels of exuberance. Scott was a man of tremendous energy both as a prominent Scottish political figure as well as an immensely popular writer who gave us *Ivanhoe, Rob Roy, and The Lady of the Lake.* He suffered from polio as a young child and remained lame, walking with a limp throughout his life although it did not prevent him, as described by close friend and fellow fell-walker William Wordsworth, from joyfully scampering along the treacherous Stridling Ridge atop the Cumbrian Mountain Helvellyn. He certainly can *fill the fife* (a small flute used with the drum in military bands) with his joy for life.

Matsuo Basho was the most famous poet of the Edo period in Japan and a great master of haiku. After years of teaching and fame, he moved from urban life and literary circles to wander the countryside taking his inspiration from first hand experiences of nature. With the simplest of noticing Basho encapsulates the very image of a creature intoxicated with the sweetness of life.

Numbers
Mary Cornish b. 1948

I like the generosity of numbers.
The way, for example,
they are willing to count
anything or anyone:
two pickles, one door to the room,
eight dancers dressed as swans.

I like the domesticity of addition—
add two cups of milk and stir—
the sense of plenty: six plums
on the ground, three more

falling from the tree.

And the multiplication's school
of fish times fish,
whose silver bodies breed
beneath the shadow
of a boat.

Even subtraction is never loss,
just addition somewhere else:
five sparrows take away two,
the two in someone else's
garden now.

I happened upon this marvelous poem of positivity and buoyancy in *Poetry 180 A Turning Back to Poetry,* an Anthology of Poems edited by Billy Collins[5] and I immediately felt cheered. Voila! The joy of being in the realm of the positive outlook and sanguine humor of the Type Seven realm, present in some degree (however deeply buried) in all of us. I found myself reading it over and over, silently and aloud and even trying to sing it (no one was in the room) as my mood lifted and I felt glad to be there in that single moment in the company of such a work of art. Thank you Mary Cornish, who after years as an author and illustrator of Children's books, tragically developed a progressive malady affecting her drawing hand and (not giving up, I may point out) moved on to creative writing, "coming to poetry late in my life." We are all richer for her decision to move forward.

---

[5] Poetry 180 A Turning Back to Poetry, edited by Billy Collins, 2003 Random House, Inc.

Kubla Khan
Samuel Taylor Coleridge (1772-1834)

In Xanadu did Kubla Khan
  A stately pleasure-dome decree:
where Alph, the sacred river, ran
Through caverns measureless to man
   Down to a sunless sea.
So twice five miles of fertile ground
With walls and towers were girdled round:
And here were gardens bright with sinuous rills,
Where blossomed many an incense-bearing tree,
And here were forests ancient as the hills,
Enfolding sunny spots of greenery.
....

This visit to Xanadu form the famous opening lines of Samuel Taylor Coleridge's richly imagined poem which, according to the story he often told, was composed entirely amidst a dream from which he was rudely awakened by a pounding upon his door. I include it here for it was written by the romantic, creative genius and terribly flawed idealist, critic, philosopher and poet who, with huge energy and restlessness, lived a life teetering between spectacular creative output and dissolute irresponsibility. Coleridge, renowned for his sparkling conversation and charm, got by his entire life with both his genius and the help of his friends, William Wordsworth being one of his closest, until he descended into depression and dependency on opium which he dissolved in brandy. He abandoned his wife and children to be cared for by family and friends, and lived his life sallying forth for new experiences and a kind of fleeing from anything restraining his freedom. Here in Xanadu, he created his longed-for pleasure-dome and a magnificent pleasure palace it is. I include these stunning lines as the unfortunate metaphor for the poet's life: an unending search for the 'imagined' pleasure-dome never to have fully realized the tangible pleasures about him.

An Alarm Clock Powered by AAA Batteries
Brad Leithauser b. 1953

Two slender bodies are the fuel
It feeds upon. You might suppose them dead
And buried, but their hearts are beating . . .
Witness the blood-bright light they shed.
It's the sheer steadiness of appetite —
Never a moment when the thing's not eating —
That chills you in the dead of night.
Time isn't just unjust but cruel.

When I first read this poem in Leithauser's 'light poetry' volume "Toad to Nightingale" I was stunned, the way you are when you get an unexpected zing of a shock when touching an electrically charged surface. Light verse? But then some of the greatest lessons come delivered with such a shock, to wake us up and ask us to look a bit deeper at our experience. We are asked to see *blood-bright* light which should tip us off, but it is the line *It's the sheer steadiness of appetite* that thrust me forward into the ravenous energy of the Type Seven as appetite outstrips much else. We end chilled in the dead of night instead of comforted by the warmth of the light. Think about it.

Sonnet 129
William Shakespeare (1564-1616)

The expense of spirit in a waste of shame
Is lust in action; and, till action, lust
Is perjured, murderous, bloody, full of blame,
Savage, extreme, rude, cruel, not to trust,
Enjoy'd no sooner but despised straight;
Past reason hunted, and no sooner had,
Past reason hated as a swallowed bait
On purpose laid to make the taker mad;
Mad in pursuit, and in possession so;
Had, having, and in quest to have, extreme;
A bliss in proof, and proved, a very woe,
Before, a joy proposed; behind, a dream.
    All this the world well knows, yet none knows well
    To shun the heaven that leads men to this hell.

Here we have Shakespeare in perhaps his darkest mood calling out the human tendency in each of us, but most dangerously in the Type Seven who loses touch with his or her finer self, toward the temptation to lust, hunt, pursue, possess and before he or she knows it the joy is left behind, only a dream. And with this ceaseless compulsion, to want, to pursue, to have he or she ends in shunning a heavenly peace for an agitated hell. A grim thought to see how one can take one's finest gift and turn it to woe.

Odes II, 10
Horace (65-8 BCE) translated by William Cowper (1731-1800)

Receive, dear friend, the truths I teach,
So shalt thou live beyond the reach

Of adverse fortune's power,
Not always tempt the distant deep,
Nor always timorously creep
Along the treacherous shore.

He that holds fast the golden mean,
And lives contentedly between
the little and the great,
Feels not the wants that pinch the poor,
Nor plagues that haunt the rich man's door,
Imbittering all his state.

The tallest pines feel most the power
Of wintry blast, the loftiest tower
Comes heaviest to the ground;
The bolts that spare the mountain's side,
His cloud-capt eminence divide
And spread the ruin round.

The well-inform'd philosopher
Rejoices with a wholesome fear,
And hopes in spite of pain;
If winter bellow from the north,
Soon the sweet spring comes dancing forth,
And nature laughs again.

What if thine heaven he overcast?
The dark appearance will not last,
Expect a brighter sky;
The God that strings the silver bow,
Awakes sometimes the Muses too,
And lays his arrows by.

If hindrances obstruct they way,
Thy magnanimity display,
And let they strength be seen;

But oh! if Fortune fill thy sail
With more than a propitious gale,
Take half thy canvas in!

Nobel Roman, Horace needs no gloss to spur you on. *Thy magnanimity display*!

Lost
David Wagoner b. 1926

Stand still. The trees ahead and bushes beside you
Are not lost. Wherever you are is called Here,
And you must treat it as a powerful stranger,
Must ask permission to know it and be known.
The forest breathes. Listen. It answers,
I have made this place around you.
If you leave it, you may come back again, saying
Here.
No two trees are the same to Raven.
No two branches are the same to Wren.
If what a tree or a bush does is lost on you,
You are surely lost. Stand still. The forest knows
Where you are. You must let it find you.

Consider the forward moving energy, the drive, the pace of the busy seeking mind of the Type Seven and ask what is most required to open space for the creativity of this joyful curiosity to blossom? Stillness. *Stand still* opens Wagoner's tranquil and rooted poem. David Wagoner is recognized as a leading poet of the Pacific Northwest and is equally lauded as novelist and creative writing teacher as he is a poet. His novels of the American West all feature a heroic protagonist who, as critic David W. Madden wrote in *Twentieth-Century Writers of the West,* his protagonists move "from innocence to experience as he journeys across the American frontier encountering an often debased and corrupted world. However, unlike those he meets, the hero retains his fundamental optimism and incorruptibility." Surely this describes the Essential Nature of the Type Seven.

In *Lost* Wagoner gives us the image of the forest as the *Here* where we may rest, ground ourselves and feel found regardless of the tumult we may experience along our journey's way. The hurry to get somewhere and somehow *know* where that somewhere is, may plague the busy searching mind of the Seven. This can end in paradoxically getting somewhere but not feeling *there* but still lost. Wagoner reminds us: Stand still and listen. The answer waits *there* which is *Here.*

We are the driving ones
Rainer Maria Rilke (1875-1926) trans. by Stephen Mitchell

We are the driving ones,
Ah, but the step of time:
think of it as a dream
in what forever remains.

All that hurrying
soon will be over with;
only what lasts can bring
us to the truth.

Young men, don't put your trust
into trails of flight,
into the hot and quick.

All things already rest:
darkness and morning light,
flower and book.

Fresh
Naomi Shihab Nye b. 1952

To move
cleanly.
Needing to be
nowhere else.
Wanting nothing
from any store.
To lift something
you already had
and set it down in
a new place.
Awakened eye
seeing freshly.
What does that do to
the old blood moving through
its channels?

Rilke and Nye, both whom we've met before in this collection bring to light a transformative pathway for the Seven part in each of us: to slow, rest, and find contentment and new possibility in what we already have at hand. And when we can do this a freshness bubbles up within. We are invited to explore the experience of our *old blood* moving through us in new way. Like the arterial blood, freshly infused with the oxygen we breathe in moment to moment, we too may slow and savor as we too are invigorated (re-oxygenated) and reawakened to live our best self.

If thou has the gift of strength, then know
Thy part is to uplift the trodden low;
Else in a giant's grasp until the end
A hopeless wrestler shall thy soul contend.
~ George Meredith from "The Burden of Strength"

Eight
The Challenger

True strength and aliveness in the moment— the knowing that we are here, rooted on this earth and are totally alive and capable of decisive and direct action is the great gift of the Type Eight temperament. It is with this strength and aliveness that the heart opens in a truly magnanimous way. It is the Eight in us that loves what is real and has a built-in lie detector for what isn't. The line from the Book of Revelation in which Jesus says "Because you are lukewarm I will spew you out" expresses the intense quality of the Eight who above all wishes to be met directly with honesty and conviction.

With the full engagement of our powerful instinctual drives, the Type Eight shows up in the world; is heard; moves into action and makes things happen. This huge energy is palpable, felt by others as a force. It contains the potential for great leadership, for inspiring the downtrodden, and for protecting those who cannot protect themselves. A genuine authority leads in contrast to an authoritarian overuse of power.

The great challenge for the Eight in all of us is how to regulate this inherent bodily strength, drop our defenses and allow in our own vulnerability. As the Eight softens the body and opens the heart great strength manifests as service to mankind.

Essential Gifts

- Strength, Aliveness, Immediacy

Focus of Attention

- Intensity and Being in control

At my Best

- I am self-confident, take initiative, make things happen
- I protect and empower others

As I lose contact with my Essential Self

- I struggle for power and dominance
- I feel that the world must adjust to me

When I've lost contact with True Nature

- I can become vengeful and ruthless
- I can become destructive to myself and others

Doorway to Growth

- Embracing my vulnerability

When you stumble and fall,
there you find pure gold.
~ Carl Jung

ODE III, 3

Horace (65 BCE-8 BCE) translated by Lord Byron

I

The man of firm, and noble soul,
No factious clamors can control;
No threatening tyrant's darkling brow,
Can swerve him from his just intent,
Gales the warring waves which plow,
By Auster on the billows spent,
To curb the Adriatic main,
would awe his fix'd determined mind in vain.

II

Aye, and the red right arm of Jove,
Hurtling his lightnings from above,
With all his terrors there unfurl'd,
He would, unmoved, gnaw'd, behold;
The flames of an expiring world,
Again in crashing chaos roll'd
In vast promiscuous ruin hurl'd,
Might light his glorious funeral pile,
Still dauntless midst the wreck of earth he'd smile.

Horace (Quintus Horatius Flaccus) was the leading Roman lyric poet at the time of Augustus during the great transition of Rome from Caesar's Republic to the age of Empire. It was a time of fierce battles culminating in the famous Battle of Philippi in 42AD where Augustus, then Octavian, defeated his great foe Marc Antony. Great forces moved, challenging the status quo and changing the face of Rome for a thousand years to come.

Horace, the son of a freed slave, was educated in Rome and Athens and it was there in Greece that he learned the power of Greek Lyric Poetry. In his Odes Horace extolled high qualities and standards to be honored in the Roman citizen. Here in the first stanzas of the Ode perseverance and strength embody the powerful presence of one standing firm with purpose, despite the *Gales on warring waves*, and the winds (*Auster* is the name given the moist South Wind) buffeting the Coast of the Adriatic sea, a sea so often the site of great Roman Naval battles.

Jove, also known as Jupiter, was the Chief God of the Romans, analogous to Zeus for the Greeks. Jove was the God of the Sky and Thunder and is pictured with an eagle at his side and a thunderbolt in his hand. He is power and strength and courage as seen in the true leader — the challenger who is deterred by nothing and can stand firmly, *dauntless midst the wreck of earth* and smile, not from joy but from knowing that he has stood firm and met the challenge.

Notice this ancient poet's choice of words as translated by the equally famous Lord Byron, great romantic poet of the 18th Century. *Firm*, and *noble*, and taking *control*; *gales* and *awe* with his *fix'd* determined mind and ultimately dauntless in his *just intent*. There is no better description of the strength of the Type Eight than this standing strong in service of one's just intent.

I Am the Poet
Walt Whitman (1836-1902)

I am the poet of reality
I say the earth is not an echo
Nor man an apparition;
But that all the things seen are real,
The witness and albic dawn of things equally real

I have split the earth and the hard coal and rocks and the solid bed
of the sea
and went down to reconnoitre there a long time,
And bring back a report,
And I understand that those are positive and dense every one
And that what they seem to the child they are
And that the world is not a joke,
Nor any part of it a sham.

Knowing and seeking what is alive, real, and present in the moment is the domain of the type Eight. Doing and speaking directly are high values for this temperament as the wonderfully alive Walt Whitman exemplified in his life and work. He tells us directly and with a kind of intense clarity: *I am the poet of reality.* He invites us to his and our world, palpably rooted as *the hard coal and rocks and the solid bed of the sea.* He asks us to feel the grounding beneath our feet. Fully present in the moment, direct, real— Walt Whitman reminds us what is accessible for us all.

The Reveille
Bret Harte (1836-1902)
A Poem Published during the Civil War

Hush! I hear the tramp of thousands,
And of armed men the hum;
Lo! a nation's hosts have gathered
Round the quick-alarming drum,—
Saying: "Come,
Freeman, come!
Ere your heritage be wasted," said the quick-alarming drum.

"Let me of my heart take counsel;
War is not of life the sum;
Who shall stay and reap the harvest
When the autumn days shall come?
But the drum
Echoed: "Come!
Death shall reap the braver harvest," said the solemn-sounding drum.

"But when won the coming battle,
What of profit springs therefrom?
What if conquest, subjugation,
Even greater ills become?"
But the drum
Answered: "Come!
You must do the sum to prove it," said the Yankee-Answering drum.

"What if, mid the cannons' thunder,
Whistling shot and bursting bomb
When my brothers fall around me,
Should my heart grow cold and numb?"
But the drum
Answered: "Come!
Better there in death united than in life a recreant,—Come!"

Thus they answered—hoping, fearing,
Some in faith and doubting some,
Till a trumpet voice proclaiming,
Said: "My chosen people, come!"
Then the drum,
Lo! was dumb;
For the great heart of the nation, throbbing, answered: "Lord, we come!"

During the furious fight for the abolition of slavery amidst America's Civil War, Bret Harte, California journalist and close friend of Mark Twain wrote these lines, first published in a California newspaper. They were written directly to touch the everyday individual struggling to face the ambivalence of a war waged between brothers.

Feel the aliveness, the energy, the command for action. In his repeating call to hear the *quick-alarming drum* enlivening us to *Come, Freeman, come!* Harte pulls us into our own sense of physical vitality and presence in the moment. Try standing up, sensing your feet squarely rooted on the ground as you read these lines aloud. Feel the rhythm and beat in your body. Harte chose lines meant to awaken an aliveness in the reader. The cadence, rhythm and shape of the poem all pull us into the experience of standing firm in this highly critical moment in time. This poem is rooted in the now: demanding, commanding, leading us to a higher purpose— calling forth the Magnanimous Heart to act for Truth and Good. This is the Heart of the Eight.

For God's Sake, Let Us Sit Upon the Ground
William Shakespeare (1564-1616)

For God's sake, let us sit upon the ground,
And tell sad stories of the death of kings;
How some have been disposed; some slain in war;
Some haunted by the ghosts they have deposed;
Some poisoned by their wives; some sleeping killed;
All murdered:—for within the hollow crown
That rounds the mortal temples of a king
Keeps Death his court; and there the antick sits,
Scoffing his state, and grinning at his pomp;
Allowing him a breath, a little scene,

To monarchize, be feared, and kill with looks;
Infusing him with self and vain conceit—
As if this flesh, which walls about our life,
Were brass impregnable; and humored thus,
Comes at the last, and with a little pin
Bores through his castle-wall, and — farewell king!

William Shakespeare who the respected literary critic Harold Bloom called the great mirror of mankind[6], warns of the overuse of a leader's power and what comes of it in the voice of Richard II. Here in Act 3, Scene 2 of 'King Richard the Second' the king speaks of the temptation which lies *within the hollow crown.* When the inherent power which we all possess, but is the everyday reality of the Type Eight, begins to define us *As if this flesh, which walls about our life,/ Were brass impregnable* we are at risk of becoming completely fixated in what can feel quite like intoxicating power. Here is turning action taken with authority into authoritarian action — the wise and respected leader degenerating into the feared tyrant. Wrapped up in our own fear patterns this *brass impregnable* strength is wielded as an iron shield, blocking out any feeling of vulnerability. Joseph Stalin comes to mind here. I was surprised to learn how respected and warmly admired he was in his youth as a forceful voice for the people. History bears witness to his power's dissolution into that of a brutal and murderous despot.

Shakespeare has his king sit not elevated upon a throne but directly on terra firma to speak a warning and a truth. He, like Whitman, the 'poet of reality, minces no words. Deny our vulnerability as we

[6] *Shakespeare, The Invention of the Human*, Harold Bloom 1998 Riverhead Books

brandish our power and we run the ultimate risk of destroying all —*farewell king!*

My Papa's Waltz
Theodore Roethke (1908-1963)

The whiskey on your breath
Could make a small boy dizzy;
But I hung on like death:
Such walking was not easy.

We romped until the pans
Slid from the kitchen shelf;
My mother's countenance
Could not unfrozen itself.

The hand that held my wrist
Was battered on one knuckle;
At every step you missed
My right ear scraped a buckle.

You beat time on my head
With a palm caked hard by dirt,
Then walked me off to bed
Still clinging to your shirt.

My Papa's Waltz captures a powerful moment in time. Theodore Roethke was born in Saginaw, Michigan, the son of a German immigrant who owned greenhouses. When Roethke was just fourteen his father died and his uncle committed suicide. He was a man well acquainted with harsh reality.

A burly man who cultivated a tough bear-like image, Roethke was drawn to physical strength and was known to be fascinated by gangsters. He wrote in a plain, no frills manner which poet and writer James

Dickey called writing with a 'kind of deep, gut vitality.' He led a difficult life suffering bouts of manic depression, yet he never ceased his search for truth in life and in his writing.

We can feel his response, his 'gut vitality' as he sets the domestic scene— dancing with his father about the farmhouse kitchen, his mother looking coldly on. This was no easy household and no easy father-son bond. Yet Roethke wrote this poem directly to his father, like a danced waltz, in a lilting 3/4 time.

When I first read this poem I asked myself 'Why a waltz?' 'Why the dance which epitomizes loving embrace and joyful moving in union?' Read it aloud and feel the waltzing lilt and imagine time being beat with open palm upon a small boy's head. Here, I believe, is the subtle expression of the deep love of a father for a son in perhaps the only state (whiskey breathed) and way (moving in a small kitchen) in which this hard man whose hands are c*aked hard by dirt* can express his love. Feel the deep, visceral honor for this flawed man as Roethke writes the poem directly to his Papa, dancing for us the stupendous capacity for love enveloped in strength.

Imaginary Career
Rainer Maria Rilke (1875-1926) translated by
Stephen Mitchell

At first a childhood, limitless and free
of any goals. Ah sweet unconsciousness.
Then sudden terror, schoolrooms, slavery,
the plunge into temptation and deep loss.

Defiance. The child bent becomes the bender,
inflicts on others what he once went through.
Loved, feared, rescuer, wrestler, victor,

he takes his vengeance, blow by blow.

And now in vast, cold, empty space, alone.
yet hidden deep within the grown-up heart,
a longing for the first world, the ancient one...

Then, from His place of ambush, God leapt out.

In Rilke's *Imaginary Career* we are treated to a study in how one begins to and proceeds to armor oneself, walling off and defending a vulnerable heart against the assaults of life. It speaks to the strong physical habits that can build over time as the armor of personality grows.

Rilke, so like Walt Whitman a generation earlier, strove his entire life to seek truth and to form a deep and spiritual connection with his fellow man. He was born in Bohemia the son of an authoritarian father who sent him to a military academy at a young age. This sensitive young boy was much traumatized and escaped often into an inner world of his own imaginings. It is no wonder that he could write so experientially of this world of *vast, cold, empty space, alone* where he longs for *the first world, the ancient one.*

Note how Rilke describes this buildup of personality defense in terms of the Type Eight — the individual becomes the *bender* and *inflicts on others what he once went through* and is in turn *loved, feared* and acts *blow by blow.* Rilke's choice of words, words indicating strongly physical even violent action, reflect the Eight energy as expressed in the habits of personality. I have wondered if his father was an unhealthy Type Eight because Rilke seems all too familiar with the unhealthy aspects of this personality type.

Rilke also describes the shift to the space *hidden deep within the grown-up heart* in which he searches for his innocent original self. This same shift happens for the Eight as, when in the grip of defiance and escalating anger he or she too can stop and turn inward. This is a shift to a still place within. In this quiet, inner place guidance awaits and, as Rilke writes, sits as if *in ambush, God leapt out.* Here the huge, moving-outward physicality of the Eight quiets, turns inward, and opens to the stillness and the greater knowing of a Greater Mind. This is indeed the path of transformation for the Eight in each of us, awakening to our original and innocent self.

The Seven Streams
David Whyte b. 1955

Come down drenched, at the end of May,
with the cold rain so far into your bones
that nothing will warm you
except your own walking
and let the sun come out at the day's end
by Slievenaglasha with the rainbows doubling
over Mulloch Mor and see your clothes
steaming in the bright air. Be a provenance
of something gathered, a summation of
previous intuitions, let your vulnerabilities
walking on the cracked, sliding limestone,
be this time, not a weakness, but a faculty
for understanding what's about
to happen. Stand above the Seven Streams,
letting the deep down current surface
around you, then branch and branch
as they do, back into the mountain,
and as if you were able for that flow,
say a few necessary words

and walk on, broader and cleansed
for having imagined.

Here the doorway to a more spacious and effective life is the very opposite of establishing dominance; it is accepting our own vulnerability and feeling our wounds, letting down our defenses.

In *The Seven Streams* David Whyte brings us to the foot of Mulloch Mor (Irish for *great hilltop)* at the close of a cold spring day as the sun comes out and warms our chilled bones. He suggests that we learned something valuable high atop this fell and he reminds us to *let your vulnerabilities/walking on the cracked, sliding limestone,/be this time, not a weakness, but a faculty/for understanding what's about/to happen.* This is the invitation for the Eight in all of us.

He goes on to invite us to be nourished by what has happened to us high up in the hills, a lovely metaphor for all the obstacles we have surmounted along our own individual journeys — to be 'able,' the Irish word for the capacity to 'do' something. In the imagery of seven flowing streams coming together at the mountain's base, Whyte shows us likewise that we too can gather such currents of power flowing from deep within and harness tremendous force to walk on, *broader and cleansed/ for having imagined.*

Courageous Vulnerability
Jamie K. Reaser

I want for you
courageous vulnerability.

Please sit for awhile and listen
to the ferocious whisperings
of my heart, and yours.

How can it be so frightening
to tenderly touch below this skin
which cloaks us so temporarily?

I once came face to face with a mystic
who taught me to cascade love
through our eyes
on the wavelength of intent.

It was simultaneously
terrifying
and rapturous.

Nothing has appeared dull since.

I want this for you...

this endless intimate gaze and glint.

I want for you the conviction
of a firm and open stance –

to be a heart warrior
who welcomes the piercing
of Life's blade
at the hands of the Beloved.

May you be met in your bloodletting
by those who
know what it is to
surrender victoriously.

I want this for you.

This, and nothing else,

is the full celebration of
our humanity.

In this last poem by Jamie K. Reaser, conservation ecologist, communication psychologist and award winning contemporary poet we are offered an invitation to enter a passageway through which lies growth and the possibility for transformative change. Its key is letting down our guard as we acknowledge our own vulnerability. We may then see with eyes afresh the courage of our heart deep within. May you savor the journey.

One could do worse than be a
swinger of birches.
~ Robert Frost,
from *'Birches'*

Three
The Achiever

How do we actually *do* our work in the world? It is the Three in us that shows us how — how to, with an open heart, bring our greatest gifts to others. Often referred to as the Masters of Effectiveness of the Enneagram, the healthy Type Three navigates life with fluidity and adaptability, bringing value to all that they do. Consider Oprah, a truly Type Three heroine of our time, and what she accomplishes as she inspires and motivates others to live from their highest self.

Healthy Threes have a magnetic force that shines out and touches others. They are expert at doing what needs to be done to accomplish a goal. The entire Olympic Games are predicated on Three energy— steadfast hard work preparing to do one's absolute best in the moment. The rub comes in for the Three when the goal overtakes the means and their huge outward energy goes on overdrive, potentially warping rules and ethics in pursuit of the prize. I recall a former patient who was a high driving, top of her field saleswoman who presented with Chronic Fatigue Syndrome. She hadn't taken a vacation in five years — "No time to slow down," she told me. She literally burned herself out. This, I believe, can be the cost of overusing one's gift. The invitation for the Three in all of us is to slow down, open our hearts to our essential worth and let our great capacity shine unencumbered as we do our life's work.

Essential Gifts

- Glory in being a valuable human being inspiring others

Focus of Attention

- How I am seen for success

At my Best

- I am competent and hard working
- I have high self-esteem which motivates others

As I lose contact with my Essential Self

- I become overly competitive
- I am driven for success

When I've lost contact with True Nature

- I can become desperate to impress others
- I can become deceitful and arrogant

Doorway to Growth

- Slowing down and opening my heart to my true value

In stillness and in rest shall be your strength.
~ Isaiah 30:15

Lines from The Prelude, Book I
William Wordsworth (1770-1850)

Dust as we are, the immortal spirit grows
Like harmony in music; there is a dark
Inscrutable workmanship that reconciles
Discordant elements, makes them cling together
In one society. How strange, that all
The terrors, pains, and early miseries,
Regrets, vexations, lassitudes interfused
Within my mind, should e'er have borne a part,
The calm existence that is mine when I
Am worthy of myself! Praise to the end!

The great knowing of the Type Three is how to use oneself well in this world. How to use one's gifts of caring through doing in the most heartfelt way possible. We are .created with a *dark/Inscrutable workmanship that reconciles/Discordant elements* Wordsworth writes, describing I think the mysterious makeup of our body, mind, and spirit in order to bring our efforts, through all the adversity — *Regrets, vexations, lassitudes* — to a functioning that is worthy of our creation. It is what Enneagram scholar and teacher Russ Hudson would call 'walking in our glory.' In his great thirteen book autobiographical poem *The Prelude* Wordsworth traces the development of his creative mind and the maturation of his capacities to write poetry touching on the core Essence of man and his place here in mortal flesh. Having spent many months now, over a period of years living just a few miles from Wordsworth's home in the Lake District in the far north of England, I can feel the support of the landscape he so loved and the freshness of the mountain air and flowing becks which nurtured him in bringing his most worthy self to me, to us. *Praise to the end!*

The Fish, the Man, and the Spirit
Leigh Hunt (1784-1859)

TO A FISH

You strange, astonished-looking, angle-faced,
  Dreary-mouthed, gaping wretches of the sea,
  Gulping salt-water everlastingly,
Cold-blooded, though with red your blood be graced,
And mute, though dwellers in the roaring waste;
  And you, all shapes beside, that fishy be,—
  Some round, some flat, some long, all devilry,
Legless, unloving, infamously chaste:—

O scaly, slippery, wet, swift, staring wights,
  What is't ye do? What life lead? eh, dull goggles?
How do ye vary your vile days and nights?
  How pass your Sundays? Are ye still but joggles
In ceaseless wash? Still nought but gapes, and bites,
  And drinks, and stares, diversified with boggles?

THE FISH ANSWERS

AMAZING monster! that, for aught I know,
  With the first sight of thee didst make our race
  For ever stare! O flat and shocking face,
Grimly divided from the breast below!
Thou that on dry land horribly dost go
  With split body and most ridiculous pace,
  Prong after prong, disgracer of all grace,
Long-useless-finned, haired, upright, unwet, slow!
O breather of unbreathable, sword-sharp air,
  How canst exist? How bear thyself, thou dry

And dreary sloth? What particle canst share
Of the only blessed life, the watery?
I sometimes see of ye an actual *pair*
Go by! linked fin by fin! most odiously.

THE FISH TURNS INTO A MAN, AND THEN INTO A SPIRIT, AND AGAIN SPEAKS

Indulge thy smiling scorn, if smiling still,
O man! and loathe, but with a sort of love:
For difference must its use by difference prove,
And sweet clang, the spheres with music fill.
One of the spirits am I, that at his will
Live in whate'er has life—fish, eagle, dove—
No hate, nor pride, beneath nought, nor above,
A visitor of the rounds of God's sweet skill.

Man's life is warm, glad, sad, 'twixt loves and graves,
Boundless in hope, honoured with pangs austere,
Heaven-gazing; and his angel-wings he craves:—
The fish is swift, small-needing, vague yet clear,
A cold, sweet, silver life, wrapped in round waves,
Quickened with touches of transporting fear.

How am I seen? We all have this Type Three preoccupation alive in us to some degree. And how do we judge others by what we see? Leigh Hunt, English lyrical poet of the Romantic movement in England wrote many satirical poems, this ditty being my favorite. Hunt was an astute observer of human behavior and of human talent and equally generous in his efforts to bring young writers to the public's attention, including Keats, Browning, Shelley, Tennyson, and Charles Dickens. John Keats thought so highly of him that he dedicated his volume *Poems Published in 1817* to him with a Dedication ending in the lines ... *I feel a free,/A leafy luxury, seeing I could please/ With these poor offerings, a man like thee.*

His keen eye and cheerful wit make his poems accessible while still thought- provoking. Notice how man asks the fish *What is't ye do? What life lead?* How often do we approach someone or something different from ourselves with this initial query. Something to think and reflect upon as we crave our *angel-wings* and do our part to earn them.

True Rest

Johann Wolfgang von Goethe (1749-1832)

Rest is not quitting
    The busy career,
Rest is the fitting
    of self to one's sphere.

'Tis the brook's motion,
    Clear without strife,
Fleeting to ocean,
    After this life.

'Tis loving and serving,
    The highest and best;
'Tis onward unswerving,
    And this is true rest.

A famous quote by Goethe, brilliant German statesman and author of *Faust,* is as follows: "Knowing is not enough; we must apply. Willing is not enough; we must do." This so perfectly reflects the Type Three's extraordinarily superior capacity 'to do.' Notice how Goethe compares rest to *a brook's motion, clear without strife,* what in today's lingo might be called *going with the flow.* The flow, the *doing* with a purpose to love and serve our highest and best intentions — the worthiness of self Wordsworth so valued. The efficient, productive, and energetic Type Three gifts given wholeheartedly create an abundant stream, a flow of value and inspiration for others.

Simplex Munditiis
(In Simple Elegance)
Ben Jonson (1573-1637)

Still to be neat, still to be drest,
As you were going to a feast;
Still to be powdered, still perfumed:
Lady, it is to be presumed,
Though art's hid causes are not found,
All is not sweet, all is not sound.

Give me a look, give me a face,
That makes simplicity a grace;
Robes loosely flowing, hair as free:
Such sweet neglect more taketh me
Than all th' adulteries of art;
They strike mine eyes, but not my heart.

The prosaic proverb "Beauty is only skin deep" is nothing new, but Jonson asks us to look beneath the surface at what we so often counterfeit — our inner state in our attempts to cover it over with powders, perfumes, and *adulteries of art.* Is not the true *art* our value and glory of our Essential Nature, quite unadorned. The Type Three in us is at such high risk to fall prey to confusing the adornment with the real thing. For what really touches the heart?

Ben Jonson was an energetic playwright, actor, poet, literary critic and political satirist. He enjoyed the patronage of King James I yet often found himself in hot water after inserting objectionable (at least to the Royal point of view) comments in his plays. Scottish by birth, he spent time in Scotland in 1619 with his dear friend Scottish poet William Drummond who, in his diary in which he strove to record as much of their conversation together as he could, preserved a flavor of Jonson's personality. I find it curious that Drummond described Jonson as "a great lover and praiser of himself." Perhaps this poem was a reminder to Jonson himself as well as to his reader. Old habits die very, very hard indeed.

Two Bears

Hafiz (1315-1390) translated by Daniel Ladinsky

Once
After a hard day's forage
Two bears sat together in silence
On a beautiful vista
Watching the sun go down
And feeling deeply grateful
For life.

Though, after a while
A thought-provoking conversation began
Which turned to the topic of
Fame.

The one bear said,
"Did you hear about Rustam?
He has become famous
And travels from city to city
In a golden cage;

He performs to hundreds of people

Who laugh and applaud
His carnival
Stunts."

The other bear thought for
A few seconds

Then started
Weeping.

In our drive to achieve, to succeed, to be recognized and to be applauded, how far do we go? What is the cost of *fame?* This is a very Type Three trap into which I imagine we have all fallen, at least a time or two. Do we see the cage for the gold? Hafiz was a master of simplicity as he touched upon the passions of human endeavor. He so artfully and humorously entreats us to examine this passion within our own personalities. For the Type Three it becomes the clear and present danger.

The Need to Win
Chuang Tzu ' Zhuangzi' (370- 287 BCE) trans. by Thomas Merton

When an archer is shooting for nothing
He has all his skill.
If he shoots for a brass buckle
He is already nervous.
If he shoots for a prize of gold
He goes blind
Or sees two targets—
He is out of his mind!

His skill has not changed. But the prize
Divides him. He cares.

He thinks more of winning
Than of shooting—
And the need to win
Drains him of power.

Try reading this poem in one long breath. It was composed by the great Chinese philosopher and poet who lived during the height of ancient Chinese philosophy. Feel the movement and breath you expend — a purposeful structure I believe he chose to reflect his message. Trying too hard for the prize we may lose the true worth of what we seek to create. Twentieth Century poet Mary Oliver has sagely advised "working for the harvest instead of the profit."[7] Chuang Tzu asks us to clarify what the goal is — the prize or the sheer display of one's skill.

Blue Girls
John Crowe Ransom (1888-1974)

Twirling your blue skirts, traveling the sward
Under the towers of your seminary,
Go listen to your teachers old and contrary
Without believing a word.

Tie the white fillets then about your lustrous hair
And think no more of what will come to pass
Than bluebirds that go walking on the grass
And chattering on the air.

Practice your beauty, blue girls, before it fail;
And I will cry with my loud lips and publish
Beauty which all our power shall never establish,
It is so frail.

---

[7] *Blue Pastures,* Mary Oliver, 1991 Harcourt, Inc. pg 59

For I could tell you a story which is true:
I know a lady with a terrible tongue,
Blear eyes fallen from blue,
All her perfections tarnished — and yet it is not long
Since she was lovelier than any of you.

I found this poem in the marvelous book "How Does a Poem Mean?"[8] by John Ciardi who, like John Crowe Ransom, was a scholar and poet, and in addition a highly respected translator of Dante's *Divine Comedy*. Ciardi pointed out the unusual choice of Ransom's words like *publish* and *establish,* pointing to their Latin roots referring to 'making public' and 'making stable.' We find these words that barely seem to fit the initial imagery of young women *traveling the sward* [moving across an expanse of short grass] amidst the swirling, driving forward movement of Ransom's sentences. Be sure to read this one aloud and feel the movement on your tongue and before long I daresay you will be swaying and twirling as if you too were whirling along.

I've chosen this poem because it brings the energy and feel of what the Type Three temperament can so easily get swept into: being dazzling, drawing attention, and being seen and admired, as with one's *lustrous hair.* Our narrator builds on his warning that 'Beauty,' at least external, is *so frail.* When time wears away the luster, where stunning eyes become those of the old woman with cataract, *blear eyes fallen from blue,* the depth of authentic beauty may be seen. Perhaps an old proverb, but here with the power of word choice, meter, and poignant image we feel punched in the gut. We get it, not on an intellectual

[8] *How does A Poem Mean?* John Ciardi, 1959 Houghton Mifflin Co. pg 802-803

level, but on a deeply felt and instinctual level— thus the power of a carefully crafted poem.

The World is Too Much With Us; Late and Soon
William Wordsworth (1770-1850)

The world is too much with us; late and soon
Getting and spending, we lay waste our powers:
Little we see in Nature that is ours;
We have given our hearts away, a sordid boon!
The Sea that bares her bosom to the moon;
The winds that will be howling at all hours,
And are up-gathered now like sleeping flowers;
For this, for everything, we are out of tune;
It moves us not—Great God! I'd rather be
A pagan suckled in a creed outworn;
So might I, standing on this pleasant lea,
Have glimpses that would make me less forlorn;
Have sight of Proteus rising from the sea;
Or hear old Triton blow his wreathed horn.

Certainly in a dark and pensive mood, here Wordsworth feels the loss of what he sees first in his young self, and also in others: the laying waste of one's powers as we give our heart away — that is, our most true and valuable gifts — as we go about *Getting and spending.* When achievement, recognition, and winning trump the expression of our greatest value, then we do as Wordsworth's image evokes, like *The winds that will be howling at all hours,/And are up-gathered now like sleeping flowers.* In giving away our heart, our finest value, we are truly at risk for living *out of tune.*

Mameen
David Whyte b. 1955

Be infinitesimal under that sky, a creature
even the sailing hawk misses, a wraith
among the rocks where the mist parts slowly.

Recall the way mere mortals are overwhelmed
by circumstance, how great reputations
dissolve with infirmity and how you,
in particular, stand a hairsbreadth from losing
everyone you hold dear.

Then, look back down the path to the north,
the way you came, as if seeing
your entire past and then south
over the hazy blue coast as if present
to a broad future.

Remember the way you are all possibilities
you can see and how you live best
as an appreciator of horizons,
whether you reach them or not.

Admit that once you have got up
from your chair and opened the door,
once you have walked out into the clean air
toward that edge and taken the path up high
beyond the ordinary, you have become
the privileged and the pilgrim,
the one who will tell the story
and the one, coming back
from the mountain,
who helped to make it.

In an online blog 'The Poetic Narrative of our Times" written a month after 9/11 David Whyte said this of poetry: "At the center of our lives, in the midst of the busyness and the forgetting, is a story that makes sense when everything extraneous has been taken away. This is poetry's province; a form of deep memory; a place from which to witness the intangible, unspeakable thresholds of incarnation we misname an average life."

For the Type Three in each of us, when we are *overwhelmed by circumstance* and our great reputations can *dissolve with infirmity,* the question is posed: Can we then remember the way we are all possibilities, looking out and stepping out beyond the image of ourselves. Here we meet transformation, or to use a favorite David Whyte word *transfiguration.* Can we strip away self-image to seek the real, the genuine, the true heart value of our essential self? Beneath the presence of this mountain Mameen in the Conomara Irish countryside we are dwarfed and perhaps a bit spooked, becoming *wraiths/among the rocks where the mist part slowly.* Whyte poses the question each of us is invited to answer: Are we *able* to live authentically.

Postscript
Seamus Heaney (1939-2013)

And some time make the time to drive out west
Into County Clare, along the Flaggy Shore,
In September or October, when the wind
And the light are working off each other
So that the ocean on one side is wild
With foam and glitter, and inland among stones
The surface of a slate-grey lake is lit
By the earthed lightning of a flock of swans.

Their feathers roughed and ruffling, white on white,
Their fully grown headstrong-looking heads
Tucked or cresting or busy underwater.
Useless to think you'll park and capture it
More thoroughly. You are neither here or there,
A hurry through which known and strange things pass
As big soft buffetings come at the car sideways
And catch the heart off guard and blow it open.

I've chosen to end this chapter, as well as the chapters of all of the nine Types with this marvelous poem by Irish poet Seamus Heaney. I found it first in Robert Hass' Anthology *Poet's Choice - Poems for Everyday Life*[9] where he introduced the poem by quoting from Heaney's 1995 Nobel Prize acceptance speech in which the poet speaks of poetry that could "persuade the vulnerable part of our consciousness of its rightness."

I would ask: how does one do that? Heaney gives us the answer with the startling last line, with the open heart, the true center of our knowing. The vivid images of Nature he observes prime us, but the answer is not *there*, but *here* in our own hearts: here on the *Flaggy Shore* in County Clare, amidst autumn winds *As big soft buffetings come at the car sideways/And catch the heart off guard and blow it open.*

No matter our personality type, our long-held and encrusted self-image, our upbringing, our traumas, our successes, or merely our everyday life; we each have within us the pure heart just waiting to be blown wide open.

---

[9] *Poet's Choice - Poems for Everyday Life,* Robert Hass, 1998 Ecco Press pg 194

Final Offerings

Along the rough road of any journey worth taking we encounter many an obstacle, at times so discouraging that we are tempted to abandon the entire project. Be they inner critic voices, or the all-too-influential comments from our loved ones or peers, or even the ever-present cultural messages of what defines value; we are lambasted, it feels at times at least, from all sides. I offer here a few more poems in support of finding your place to settle, to ground, to rest in your true self and call forth the courage to accept love as the final answer.

I met Helen Marshall the first winter I lived in the Lake District, home of Wordsworth and Coleridge. In St. John's Anglican Church in Keswick she led contemplative studies and during services she held a peaceful and steady presence, a quiet solidity I desperately needed during a tumultuous time in my life. Patti Tronolone came into my life as a Reiki master in Taos, New Mexico. Her healing hands and energy work opened gorgeous sleuths in my healing soul. Shakespeare needs no introduction and as for Shelly, oh how I wish I could have been part of his circle; yet, with his words put to paper I can absorb his essence even now centuries later.

I feel that each poem speaks for itself. I tender each as a prayer for you.

Prayer; Coming Home
Rev. Helen Marshall b. 1963

Rooted and grounded; the depth in the shallows;
the way trodden with friends; a comfortable chair;
sustenance and shock of familiar words;

the sharp relief of being known;
closing my eyes and not wanting to
see; a hard question; a deaf and dumb
mind; fear and frustration; a
self-absorbed bog; lost in the stuckness of self;
a hidden light; fresh bread;
a still pool; waiting; the cleansing
joy of tears; a vast and open
silence; wide vista of grace;
rich aloneness with all, held in the three;
presence in the now; the short journey home.

~ ~ ~

The Quality of Mercy
William Shakespeare (1564-1616)

The quality of mercy is not strained.
It droppeth as the gentle rain from heaven
Upon the place beneath. It is twice blest:
It blesseth him that gives and him that takes.
'Tis mightiest in the mightiest; it becomes
The thronèd monarch better than his crown.
His scepter shows the force of temporal power,
The attribute to awe and majesty
Wherein doth sit the dread and fear of kings;
But mercy is above this sceptered sway.
It is enthronèd in the hearts of kings;
It is an attribute to God Himself;
And earthly power doth then show likest God's
When mercy seasons justice. Therefore, Jew,
Though justice be thy plea, consider this:
That in the course of justice none of us
Should see salvation. We do pray for mercy,
And that same prayer doth teach us all to render
The deeds of mercy.

If I Could Learn the Word for Yes

Dedicated to WS Merwin, "The Child"
Patti Tronolone b. 1952

If I could learn the word for yes
And could plant it like a tall tree between my heart and my lips
I could perchance bypass
The disaster of opposition
Crowing out the myriad of unknown things.

Perhaps I would learn the language of volcanoes or
Overhear the fish
Whispering of their secret lives below the sea.

What kinds of moments would open up, uncensored?
What flowers would suddenly bloom the planet had never known?
What life would begin to leap that now only crawls?

If I could learn the word for **yes.**

Love's Philosophy
Percy Bysshe Shelley (1792-1822)

The fountains mingle with the river
　And the rivers with the ocean;
The winds of heaven mix forever
　With a sweet emotion;
Nothing in the world is single;
　All things by a law divine
In one spirit meet and mingle.
　Why not I with thine?

See the mountains kiss high heaven,

And the waves clasp one another;
No sister-flower would be forgiven
If it disdained its brother;
And the sunlight clasps the earth,
And the moonbeams kiss the sea.
What are all these kissings worth
If thou kiss not me?

Index of Poets

K

L

M

N

O

P

R

S

T

W

Y

Recommended Reading

Books About Learning the Enneagram and Understanding its Application Across Differing Disciplines

Personality Types, Don Richard Riso with Russ Hudson, 1996

Understanding the Enneagram, Don Richard Riso and Russ Hudson, 2000

Wisdom of the Enneagram, Don Richard Riso and Russ Hudson, 1999

Deep Coaching, Roxanne Howe-Murphy, EdD, 2007

Deep Living, Roxanne Howe-Murphy, EdD, 2013

The Essential Enneagram: The Definitive Personality Test and Self-Discovery Guide, David Daniels, M.D. and Virginia Price, PhD, 2012

The Spiritual Dimension of the Enneagram, Sandra Maitri, 2000

The Enneagram: A Christian Perspective, Richard Rohr and Andreas Ebert, 2013

Roaming Free Inside the Cage: A Daoist Approach to the Enneagram and Spiritual Transformation, William M. Schafer, PhD, 2009

The Enneagram and Kabbalah, Rabbi Howard A. Addison, 1998

Books About Reading Poetry

How Does A Poem Mean? John Ciardi, 1960

A Poetry Handbook, Mary Oliver, 1994

The Sounds of Poetry, Robert Pinsky, 1998

The Discovery of Poetry, Frances Mayes, 2001

Outstanding Edited and Annotated Anthologies

A Treasury of Great Poems, English and American, Louis Untermeyer, 1942

Poet's Choice: Poems for Everyday Life, Robert Hass, 1998

The Best Poems of the English Language, Harold Bloom, 2004

Stressed Unstressed: Classic Poems to Ease the Mind, Jonathan Bate and Paula Bryne, 2016

Sources and Permissions

Every effort has been made to contact copyright holders; in the event of an omission or error the editor should be notified at Sassafras Press, 822 Hartz Way #205, Danville, CA 94526.

Basho, "A bee staggers," from *The Essential Haiku: Visions of Basho, Buson, and Issa* by Robert Hass. Copyright 1993 Ecco; Bloodaxe Books, 2013 Reprinted by iPublishers and in the UK by Bloodaxe Books.

Valerie Berry, "first lesson," from *difficult news, Copyright*© 2001 by Valerie Berry, published by Sixteen Rivers Press. Permission kindly granted by the author.

David Budbill, "The Three Goals" from *Moment to Moment: Poems of a Mountain Recluse.* Copyright © 1999 by David Budbill. Reprinted with the permission of The Permissions Company, Inc., on behalf of Copper Canyon Press, www.coppercanyonpress.org

Billy Collins, "Introduction to Poetry," from *The Apple that Astonished Paris.* Copyright © 1988, 1996 by Billy Collins. Reprinted with the permission of The Permissions company, Inc., on behalf of the University of Arkansas Press, **www.uapress.com**. "Reaper" and "Genius," from THE TROUBLE WITH POETRY: AND OTHER POEMS by Billy Collins, Copyright © 2005 by Billy Collins. used by permission of Random House, an imprint and division of Penguin Random House LLC. All rights reserved.

Mary Cornish, "Numbers," from *Red Studio. Copyright* © 2007 by Mary Cornish. Reprinted by permission of Oberlin College Press, 2007.

Danna Faulds, "Maybe Not," from *From Root to Bloom: Yoga Poems and Other Writings.* Copyright © by Danna Faulds 2006. Published by Peaceable Kingdom Books. Permission kindly granted by the author.

Thom Gunn, "Baby Song," from *Jack Straw's Castle.* Copyright © 1976 by Thom Gunn. First published by Faber Library, Faber, England. Subsequently by Faber & Faber Limited, London 1993. First published in the United States in 1994 by Farrar, Straus & Giroux. Permission granted by Faber and Faber Limited and Farrar, Straus & Giroux.

Hafiz, translated by Daniel Ladinsky "Hunting Party," "It felt Love," "Crooked Deals," "Find a Better Job," "Two Bears," from *The Gift,* copyright 1999 and used with permission.

Bret Harte, "Reveille," published during the Civil War in California newspapers and magazines, first known publication in an 1882 collection of Harte's *Poems.* This poem is included in the Anthology of Civil War Poetry *"Words for the Hour"* edited by Faith Barrett and Cristanne Miller, 2005 University of Massachusetts Press

Galway Kinnell, "Blackberry Eating," from THREE BOOKS by Galway Kinnell. Copyright © 1993 by Galway Kinnell. Reprinted by permission of Houghton Mifflin Harcourt Publishing company. All rights reserved.

Brad Leithuaser, “Apple,” “Alarm Clock,” from *Toad to a Nightingale* by Brad and Mark Leithauser. Reprinted by permission of David R, Godine, Publisher, Inc. Copyright © Brad and Mark Leithauser, 2007

Denise Levertov, "Contraband," from EVENING TRAIN, copyright © 1992 by Denise Levertov. Reprinted by permission of New Directions Publishing Corp.

Derek Mahon, "Everything Is Going to Be All Right," from *New and Collected Poems (2011)* by kind permission of the author and The Gallery Press, Loughcrew, Oldcastle, County Meath, Ireland.

Amanda Mc Broom, "The Rose," song lyrics published by Alfred Music Publishing Co, Inc., Van Nuys, CA

Leslie McGrath, "Ars Poetica," from the online poetry forum *poets.org.* Used by kind permission of the author.

N.I. Negron, "Renaissance Man," published on the online poetry forum *poetrysoup.com* and winner of the Famous Painter Poetry Contest sponsored by the *poetrysoup.*

Pablo Neruda, "Planet," Summary" from *Pablo Neruda Fully Empowered,* Translated by Alastair Reed Translation copyright © 1967,1969,1970,1975 by Alastair Reid Published by arrangement with Farrar, Straus & Giroux, Inc, a division of Macmillan Publishers. Pablo Neruda “Sumario” and “Planeta”, PLENOS PODERES © 1962, Fundación Pablo Neruda.

John Frederick Nims, "Love Poem," from *The Iron Pastoral,* copyright © 1947, published by William Sloane Associates, Inc.

Naomi Shihab Nye, "Fresh," from *You & Yours,* Copyright © 2005 by Naomi Shihab Nye. Reprinted with the permission of The Permissions Company, Inc., on behalf of BOA Editions, Ltd., www.boaeditions.org. "Away Around," "If the Shoe Doesn't fit," from *A Maze Me* Copyright © 2005 by Naomi Shihab Nye. Used by permission of HarperCollins Publishers.

Mary Oliver, MOZART, FOR EAMPLE *from the volume THIRST* by Mary Oliver, published by Beacon Press, Boston - Copyright © 2006 by Mary Oliver, Used herewith by permission of the Charlotte Sheedy Literary Agency, Inc., *TODAY and POEM OF THE ONE WORLD from: A Thousand Mornings by Mary Oliver, published by The Penguin Press, New Your - Copyright* © 2012 by Mary Oliver, Used herewith by permission of the Charlotte Sheedy Literary Agency, Inc.

Dorothy Parker, "Inventory" from THE COMPLETE POEMS OF DOROTHY PARKER by Dorothy Parker, Copyright © 1999 by The National Association for the Advancement of Colored People. Used by permission of Penguin Books, an imprint of Penguin Publishing Group, a division of Penguin Random House LLC. All rights reserved.

Robert Phillips, “The Panic Bird.” *Spinach Days. P. 13.* © 2000 Robert Phillips. Reprinted with permission of Johns Hopkins University Press.

Holly Ordway, “Maps” previously appeared in *Apologetics and the Christian Imagination: An Integrated Approach to Defending the Faith,* and is reprinted here with the author’s permission.

John Crowe Ransom, "Blue Girls" from SELECTED POEMS by John Crowe Ransom, Copyright © 1924 by Alfred A. Knopf, a division of Penguin Random House LLC, copyright renewed 1952 by John Crowe Ransom. Used by permission of Alfred A. Knopf, an imprint of the Knopf Doubleday Publishing Group, a division of Penguin Random House LLC. All rights reserved.

Jamie K. Reaser, "Courageous Vulnerability" from COMING HOME: LEARNING TO ACTIVELY LOVE THIS WORLD Copyright © by Jamie K. Reaser 2015, published by Talking Waters Press. Used by the kind permission of the author.

Rainer Maria Rilke, "Buddha in Glory," translation copyright © 1982 by Stephen Mitchell; "Ah, Not To Be Cut Off," translation copyright © 1995 by Stephen Mitchell; and "Imaginary Career" from SELECTED POETRY OF RAINER MARIA RILKE by Rainer Maria Rilke, translated by Stephen Mitchell, translation copyright © 1980, 1981, 1982, by Stephen Mitchell. Used by permission of Random House, an imprint and division of Penguin Random House LLC. All rights reserved. "The Sonnets to Orpheus, II, 29," translation copyright © 1982 by Stephen Mitchell; from selected poetry of Rainer Maria Rilke, translated by Stephen Mitchell. Used by permission of Random House, an imprint and division of Penguin Random House LLC. All rights reserved. "You Darkness," translated by David Whyte from FIRE IN THE EARTH, poems by David Whyte copyright © 1992 by David Whyte, published by Many Rivers Press 2007, Langley, WA USA. Used by permission of the author. www.davidwhyte.com.

Theodore Roethke, "My Papa's Waltz," copyright © 1942 by Heart Magazines, Inc., copyright © 1966 and renewed 1994 by Beatrice Lushington; from COLLECTED POEMS by Theodore Roethke. Used by permission of Doubleday, an imprint of the Knopf Doubleday Publishing Group, a division of Penguin Random House LLC. All rights reserved.

Kay Ryan, "Patience," from SAY UNCLE by Kay Ryan, Copyright 2000 by Kay Ryan, published by Grove Atlantic New York. Reprinted by permission of Grove Atlantic, 841 Broadway, New York, NY.

Sappho, "That impossible predator" from SAPPHO, STUNG WITH LOVE translated by Aaron Poochigian Copyright © 2009 by Aaron Poochigian, first published in Penguin Classics 2009. Reprinted with additional poems 2015 by Penguin Random House UK. Permission granted by Penguin Random House UK.

Hal Sirowitz, "Lending Out Books" from MY THERAPIST SAID copyright © 1998 by Hal Sirowitz, published by Crown Publishing. Reprinted by permission of The Joy Harris Literary Agency, Inc.

Wislawa Szymborska, "A Contribution to Statistics" and "Over Wine" from POMES NEW AND COLLECTED 1957-1997 by Wislawa Szymborska, translated from the Polish by Stanislaw Baranczak and Clare Cavanagh. English translation copyright © 1998 by Houghton Mifflin Harcourt Publishing Company.

Reprinted by permission of Houghton Mifflin Harcourt Publishing Company. All rights reserved. "Returns" from SOUNDS, FEELINGS, THOUGHTS : SEVENTY POEMS by Wislawa Szymborska translated by Magnus I. Krynski and Robert A. Maguire Copyright © 1981 by Princeton University Press. Used by permission of Princeton University Press.

John Tagliabue, "Moderation is Not a Negation of Intensity, But Helps Avoid Monotony" from NEW AND COLLECTED POEMS 1997 by John Tagliabue copyright © 1997 by John Tagliabue published by the National Poetry Foundation at the University of Maine. Used by the kind permission of the National Poetry Foundation.

Patti Tronolone, "Woken in the Night by Contents Under Pressure" and "If I Could Learn the Word for Yes" from SECRET BRIGHTENING, POEMS AND PAINTINGS OF THE INNER LANDSCAPE by Patti Tronolone, copyright © 2016 by Patti Tronolone. Used by permission of the author.

David Wagoner, "Lost" from *Traveling Light: Collected and New Poems* by David Wagoner. Copyright 1999 by David Wagoner. Used with permission of the University of Illinois Press.

David Whyte, "Coleman's Bed," "Mameen," "The Seven Streams," "Tobar Phadraic," and "What to Remember When Waking,' from RIVER FLOW Copyright © 2012 by David Whyte, published by Many Rivers Press, Langley, Washington, USA. Used by permission of the author www.davidwhyte.com

CPSIA information can be obtained
at www.ICGtesting.com
Printed in the USA
FSHW02n0750230918
52479FS